The

INNER
LIGHT

The INNER LIGHT

How The Beatles
Planted the Spiritual
Seed in our Souls

JOANNE DIMAGGIO

RAINBOW RIDGE
BOOKS

The Spiritual Meaning of the Sixties by Tobias Churton published by Inner Traditions International and Bear & Company, ©2018. All rights reserved. http://www.Innertraditions.com. Reprinted with permission of publisher.

Cover and interior design by Frame25 Productions

Published by:
Rainbow Ridge Books, LLC
Virginia Beach, VA
www.rainbowridgebooks.com

Library of Congress Control Number: 2024930039

ISBN 978-1-937907-76-1

10 9 8 7 6 5 4 3 2 1
Printed in the United States of America

"I love that about the Beatles. A lot of our influences were really good—sort of spiritual, meditation, this kind of thing. I think we laid out a few paths for people to follow and it has, I think, it's had a good effect on the world. But looking back on it, it was a blessing that people picked up on it and actually helped themselves in their lives. That's a great thing."

—Paul McCartney, *McCartney 3-2-1*
His response to Paul Rubin who said the
music "changed my life only for the better."

To My Children, Marianne and Michael
And To Beatles Fans Across the Universe

Table of Contents

Acknowledgements

I want to thank everyone who took an interest in this project and added their own thoughtful insights to produce the final work:

- To Lori, who was with me in the fan club in the sixties, and who remains a friend today. Her review of the manuscript was very much appreciated.

- To all the Beatle fans who shared their thoughts on their own spiritual journey with the Fab Four, including Deborah, Gordon, Jeannie, Joy, Julie, Lisa, Nan, Susan, Doug and Rich.

- To the countless Beatle biographers whose writing supplemented, and in most instances, confirmed and embellished on the evidence I was presenting.

- To Eric Meyers and Robert Rosen for their humbling endorsements.

- To Tammy Andrews and Gabrielle Myers for edits and suggestions.

• To Lisa Marks, Patty Finlayson, Joy Scott, and others who volunteered to be readers.

I hope everyone who participated in this project, and those who have been led to read about it for the first time, will come away with a sense of understanding the influences surrounding the Beatles and our own spiritual paths.

Introduction

The Long and Winding Road

For the last thirty-seven years, I have pursued a passionate interest in reincarnation research and past-life therapy. I have written several books on the subjects of reincarnation and Soul Writing™, have been a conference presenter, a guest on numerous radio programs and podcasts, and actively involved in Edgar Cayce's Association for Research and Enlightenment (A.R.E.). I was the founder and director of my own past-life research, therapy and educational organization, called PLEXUS (Past-Life Exploration, Understanding and Sharing). I have rubbed shoulders with some of the most knowledgeable men and women in the field of reincarnation research, have done more regressions than I can count, and thanks to Zoom, now have a global clientele. So why in the world am I writing a book about the Beatles?

Don't get me wrong. I am proud of all I have accomplished, but underneath that pride is an ongoing curiosity about what influenced my life and the path I subsequently chose. It's those influences that are the real subject of the book. For me, it boils down to one puzzling question I have wrestled with for years: How did a young girl from an Italian-American Catholic family growing up in the sixties on Chicago's southside become so immersed in the world of esoteric philosophies? It always seemed so illogical—so out of place—that I couldn't rationalize it at all. I wanted an answer so I could understand the trajectory of my soul's journey in this and prior lifetimes. I know I designed this life before coming into it, but even looking at it from that perspective, I continue to wonder how did this all fall into place? More importantly, did my teenage obsession with the Beatles have anything to do with it?

There was nothing in my early years to suggest I'd become known for my work in past-life research and therapy. Certainly no one in Bridgeport, the salty neighborhood I grew up in, ever used the word "reincarnation" in a sentence, much less discussed it while sitting on their front porches in the sweltering summer heat. My mostly uneducated, blue-collar neighbors were what I secretly called, Surface Dwellers. The women would put their heavily hair-sprayed heads together to dissect the other women excluded from their circle, while the men's racist discourses generally focused on African-Americans ("they'll never move into *our* neighborhood!"), the teamster union, Mayor Richard J. Daley who lived just a few blocks up the street, or the latest criminal activity in and around the block. Stealing was commonplace and most "hot" goods were sold out in the open from the trunk of a Cadillac or Lincoln Continental.

Immigrants were terrorized. I once saw a newly arrived Italian man being chased up the middle of the street by an incensed neighbor waving a gun. This was the socioeconomic framework into which I was born.

As with any evolutionary tale, I discovered there were layers upon layers of life experiences to peel back until I got to the core to find my answer. Looking back at my adolescent and teenage years, I remember how I silently struggled with the concept of spirituality that was in opposition to what I was being taught by the Catholic Church. Simultaneously, I was contending with a feeling of alienation from my family, my friends and neighbors. If I was sure of anything, it was that I did not belong in Bridgeport, living in that two-flat brick bungalow on that tiny 25-foot lot. From a young age, I hated everything about living there. I'd walk the alleys, breathing in the stench from the garbage cans, and wonder—where are my gardens? I kept dreaming about those gardens, which was odd because we barely had a backyard, let alone a garden. What gardens? Where? When I would be among family, I found myself whispering to myself *"Who are you people?"* because on some deep level, they felt like strangers. I wanted out, but I felt trapped. I had nowhere to go and no one to confide in. Couldn't exactly bring *that* to the confessional!

Years later, I read a quotation from George Harrison that indicated he was having similar thoughts about his own life's situation: "Sometimes I feel like I'm actually on the wrong planet, and it's great when I'm in my garden, but the minute I go out the gate I think: 'What the hell am I doing here?'"

In *I Me Mine*, George reflects on his thoughts about reincarnation and how he came to grow up in Liverpool. He tried . . .

> . . . to imagine the soul entering the womb of the woman living in 12 Arnold Grove, Wavertree, Liverpool 15; there were all the barrage balloons, and the Germans bombing Liverpool. All that was going on. I sat outside the house, in the car with Olivia, a couple of years ago, imagining 1943, nipping through from the spiritual world, the astral level, getting back into a body in that house. That really is strange when you consider the whole planet, and all the planets that may be on the physical level . . . how do I come to that family in that house at that time and who am I anyway?

Interestingly, in *George Harrison: Behind the Locked Door*, author Graeme Thomson quotes George making a comment that reflected my thinking at that time in my life:

> I am conscious of the one side of 'me', which is this physical body made out of bones and flesh, that has to put on jackets and shoes and things like that; that people look at in photographs and

think, 'That's him.' I know that's 'me' when I get on an aeroplane, that's 'me' in seat six, George Harrison. But that isn't the real me. The real me is what I feel inside. George Harrison is my name for this life, but I'm not really George Harrison. There's this thing inside which isn't this person or that person, it's just a potentially pure soul that's trying to get out. In death your body falls off but you've still got two other bodies, so you go into your subtle body for a while and then you get your next physical body. You go round and round in circles, trying to get better and better. It's a learning process. Through the body, our senses, we gain experience, and through experience we gain liberation. All we have to do is try to make this moment better; each moment, try and make it a little better and then the future is going to be better.

Talking about George's detachment from the material trappings he had acquired as a famous person, Ravi Shankar, Indian sitarist, composer and George's friend, says:

It didn't seem to matter much to him, because he was searching for something much higher, much deeper. It does seem like he already had some Indian background in him. Otherwise, it's hard to explain how, from Liverpool, with his background, and then becoming so famous, what reason did he have to get so attracted to a particular type of life and philosophy, even religion? It seems very strange really. Unless you believe in reincarnation.

Unless you believe in reincarnation. Well, that explains it!

I was first introduced to reincarnation several years before the Beatles turned my world upside down. As an adolescent, my discontent with living in Bridgeport was offset by the summers I'd spend at my grandparent's cottage at Bass Lake, Indiana. We had a screened-in front porch, and it was there I began reading books by Ruth Montgomery, Jess Stearn, and other metaphysical authors. I especially gravitated to biographies of Edgar Cayce, and learned of his extraordinary gift through the 14,000+ health and life readings he gave over his lifetime.

Then there was that one summer when I found myself devouring the pages of *The Search for Bridey Murphy*, by Morey Bernstein. First published in 1956, the book chronicled how housewife, Virginia Tighe, underwent a hypnotic regression and thereafter described a life as Bridey Murphy, a woman who lived in nineteenth century Ireland. I couldn't put it down.

I can't recall a specific trigger that led me to begin reading books about reincarnation or my growing desire to learn about metaphysics, but I did know one thing, and that was to not discuss what I was reading or philosophies

I was exploring with anyone. I was fearful there would be repercussions if anyone discovered my fascination with a subject that was the antithesis of Catholic dogma. I learned to hide in plain sight.

This holding back—which I later discovered was karmic in nature and something I had done in prior lifetimes—continued well into my metaphysical career. As an example, I decided to use a variation of my maiden name (from Maggio to DiMaggio) for my professional life, while maintaining my married name for my personal life. I did this because I did not want my children to have to deal with snide remarks from their friends that their mother was a kook. Those fears no doubt were based in a prior life in which I did have that reputation! Thus, from early on, I divided those in my life into two distinct categories— my mainstream family and friends, and my metaphysical friends who, quite frankly, often felt more like my family than my biological family did.

I later learned that separation was something both John Lennon and George Harrison experienced. In *Here Comes The Sun: The Spiritual and Musical Journey of George Harrison*, author Joshua Greene writes: "George had his rock and roll friends and he had his transcendental friends, and he liked to keep them separate."

John Lennon had come to that same conclusion long before I did. Writing in *The Spiritual Meaning of the Sixties*, Tobias Churton addresses John's attitude about his beliefs versus the rest of the world: "Lamenting in 1966 following the famous 'Beatles are more popular than Jesus now' controversy with its chilling consequences worldwide, that he now felt pressured *not* to tell the truth because it was so unwelcome in the world . . . The world, John suspected, was in a kind of conspiracy against truth, especially spiritual truth, and could not be trusted."

While as a teenager I kept my metaphysical interests a secret, I had no qualms admitting I was a Beatles fan. From the moment the group arrived in the United States on February 7, 1964, I was mesmerized by them. I not only was proud of the fact that I was a Beatles fan, but I also conducted a very public, active search for fellow Beatlemaniacs—for "my people." Ironically, that need to find my particular niche was a pattern that continued throughout my life. My children would often reference my going to an esoteric conference, or hosting a program of my own, by saying: "Mom is going to be with *her* people."

The tribes may have been different in my childhood versus as an adult, but the need for connection remained the same. I never wanted to be "just" a Beatle fan, or later "just" a student of metaphysics. In both instances, I subconsciously created a catalyst that would put me in the forefront of both endeavors. My strong desire to be of service to others; to create networking opportunities so like-minded people could find each other; to act as a "reporter" and share news of interest to others through my writing— all of that compelled me to be more and do more. As a teenager, I did it through the Beatles fan club I started and ran from 1964 until 1972. As an adult, it was my active involvement in the A.R.E.

While I passionately explored the topic of reincarnation prior to the Beatles, once they came into my life, they became my single-minded allegiance and all thoughts of metaphysics vanished in favor of following the Fab Four. Back then, I never put two and two together nor gave any thought as to how one could have anything to do with the other.

So it was that in 1964 I put my interest in metaphysics on the back burner. I no longer read books on reincarnation or any other spiritual topic during the early Beatles years. I was too engrossed in growing my Beatles fan club. All that ended in 1972, when I turned my club over to someone else. After that, I lived a pretty mainstream life, married with two children, and living in a western Chicago suburb.

My closest friend at that time was Kelley. We met at a mother's support group shortly after our daughters were born in 1982, two days apart, in the same hospital. We never spoke of anything that had much substance to it, other than arranging play dates for our girls, and later for our boys who were born two years later. I liked Kelley. You might say, she represented my alter ego. Her irreverent attitude toward life appealed to me. I don't recall at first that we had much in common, other than having children the same age, so it was more a case of opposites attracting.

The Universe, however, had something specific in mind when it brought the two of us together. Five years into our friendship, we discovered something we did have in common; something that neither of us had discussed with the other. That discovery came after Shirley MacLaine's book, *Out on a Limb*, was made into a mini-series that aired on ABC, January 18-19, 1987. We both watched it, separately, and like thousands of other sleeping metaphysicians, we experienced a spiritual awakening, each in our own way. MacLaine's past-life journey intrigued me more than anything else about that series and rekindled my interest in reincarnation. Kelley was more drawn to channeling. Other than the birth of our children, those two dates in 1987 were the most significant dates in our lives.

You might say everything was flipped. As my life's focus changed to make room for those esoteric studies I had abandoned as a teenager, I did so without any thought of the Beatles. This was the complete opposite of what I did in 1964, when I let go of any interest in metaphysical topics in favor of running a Beatles fan club. Looking back, I realize now that I didn't abandon one for the other. My feet have always been planted in two different worlds—that teenage girl in the sixties who devoted her life to a rock band, and the woman in the eighties who began her true spiritual calling.

So, this brings me back to my original question: Did my deep involvement with the Beatles through the eight years I ran that fan club have anything to do with my

insatiable thirst for a deeper meaning of life? Did they sub-
liminally plant the seed that blossomed into my profound
desire to understand how the universe operated?

I believe the answer is yes. In researching material for
this book, I was struck by a statement Churton makes at
the end of his book:

> Moderation and discipline get better results, but
> one also needs spiritual strength and knowledge
> and the wisdom to apply it. In this regard, the
> Sixties marked a seedtime; the fruits are to come
> . . . The gnosis was there in seed in the Sixties.
> Embraced with moderation, determination, and
> self-discipline, it works wonders, and when the
> seeds truly flower, as they must, we may look
> forward to another astonishing—well, not a
> mere decade, but a historic era.

George was humble about the role the Beatles played
in planting those seeds. David Bennahum, writing in *In
Their Own Words: The Beatles . . . After The Break-Up*, quotes
George as saying:

> Even now I look back and I can see, relative to a
> lot of other groups or pop music in general, The
> Beatles did have something. But that's relative to
> that. Relative to something else . . . I can accept
> whatever The Beatles were on those terms. But

it's a bit too much to accept that we're supposedly the designers of this incredible change that
occurred (in the '60s). In many ways we were
just swept along with everybody else.

For many fans, that wave continued with its forward
momentum long after the Beatles ended. Our experience, our discoveries about ourselves and our perspectives
about our spiritual nature drove us into the careers we
followed years later. Candy Leonard, author of *Beatleness:
How the Beatles and Their Fans Remade the World*, writes that
many first-generation Beatle fans, a group I was firmly
entrenched in, "brought Beatleness to careers as writers,
designers, musicians, educators, therapists, social workers,
and entrepreneurs, infusing their communication with
Beatle references and sensibilities."

In her book, *A Women's History of the Beatles*, Christine
Feldman-Barrett writes: "Indeed, as fans witnessed the Beatles continuing to develop as musicians, songwriters, and
individuals during the span of their career, they too considered how one might live a dynamic and authentic life."

I wanted to explore that concept and do it from the
perspective of a former Beatles fan club president searching for greater meaning in life. I sensed I'd find a lot of
material to weave in and out of the story of my journey.
I thought most of it would be from statements made by
George rather than the other three Beatles, but when I first

started doing research for this book, I did not anticipate how lop-sided that would be.

Gary Tillery, writing in *Working Class Mystic: A Spiritual Biography of George Harrison*, called George the spiritual light that inspired the others. Tillery writes: "As a result of George's spiritual quest, elements of Eastern culture that likely would have remained exotic diversions in major cities became, with the well-publicized involvement of the Beatles, first "hip" and then acceptable to the mainstream."[1]

The premise of this book—that the Beatles planted the seed of spirituality in an entire generation—was something George had contemplated years earlier. Tillery writes that in toying with an idea for a U.S. tour in which George would devote a portion of each concert to Ravi Shankar and his musicians, the hope was this would proselytize his existing fan base:

> How many hearts and minds attracted by the aura of the Beatles could be turned toward what really mattered—Krishna? . . . If he could bring the millennia-old wisdom to the attention of the crowds who came to hear him, the curiosity of some listeners might be sparked . . . One tour might open tens of thousands of minds to the wisdom found in Eastern mysticism.[2]

And wake up, we did! And why? I have always said that Beatle fans were little sponges, soaking up whatever John,

Paul, George or Ringo said as truth. George Martin, who recorded and produced many of their albums, seems to have agreed. In the book he co-wrote, *All You Need is Ears: The Inside Personal Story of the Genius who Created the Beatles*, he stated: "Every little thing they said became translated into Beatle instruction, as to how we should behave."

Candy Leonard found that to be true as well. She quotes one Beatle fan as saying: "I didn't fully grasp it, but anything they did was ok with me." Another fan said: "Anything they did was acceptable because it was them. I never rejected anything they did."

And neither did I.

As Leonard wrote, by the time "Penny Lane" and "Strawberry Fields Forever" was released, Beatle fans felt like we were on a journey. "The destination wasn't important," she wrote. We were "challenged and enriched and wanted to stay tuned. It was doing something to them, and whatever it was, they liked it."

Many years later, writing in *Paul McCartney: The Lyrics, 1956 to Present*, Paul discusses how the group had to balance songs that interested them personally as opposed to those that the fans liked. Paul had what he called an "amazing revelation: we could be poetic without losing touch with our fans, or you might even say that the opposite occurred—that as we became more experimental and leaned more towards stream of consciousness, we actually gained fans."

There is no doubt in my mind about the tremendous influence the Beatles had on our souls. As Leonard writes, "Many said the Beatles were "imprinted" on their "spirit" or their "souls," part of their "DNA." I know this to be true just from my own spiritual journey.

Beatlemania may have appeared to be something on a surface level—a group of attractive, talented young men whose music was loved by an entire generation. Despite the early adoration that at times seemed as though it was out of control, the experience of Beatlemania proved to be much deeper than packed concert venues with screaming fans, or number one hit records. The Beatles themselves must have understood, at some point, that all of this adulation was only symptomatic of a large-scale cosmic event.

Writing in *The Spiritual Dimension of the Beatles*, author Eric Meyers addresses this underlying issue:

> It likely became apparent to them [the Beatles] that the intense reaction to Beatlemania was not really about them. It was far bigger. They were playing characters in a larger drama or process, occupying a position in an archetypal of mythological theater. A facet of the 'arc of awakening' was to stimulate the awareness of such a transpersonal perspective. It was just starting to unfold— soon, they would be more in on the game.

I kept all the Beatles fan club newsletters I published from 1964-1972 (except those lost in a flood in my parents' crawlspace), so I was able to draw on them for this book. I thought rereading those issues would give me a greater sense of what I and other fans were thinking in real time. I admit, revisiting those newsletters after having them stashed away for over a half century was a bit disconcerting. At times I cringed when I read some of the articles I wrote or published. Our naivete was on full display. I was especially disheartened by how judgmental we were about what was going on in the group's personal lives. I console myself that we were immature kids then and our worldview was less than sophisticated. So while a sharp-eyed reader may point to something and say—*well, that wasn't true*—I ask you to keep in mind that for those of us who grew up in the sixties, it *was* true because it was all the information we had. Our truth was based on what we were being fed by scrounging our limited media outlets, hungry to get whatever news we could find. This was long before the existence of the Internet, so we relied on news we'd glean from our local disc jockeys, newspapers, magazines and each other.

While the truth may have been fleeting in what we were reading and writing, our reaction to whatever was happening in the lives of the Beatles was very real. To that end, I've pulled quotes that registered our emotional thermometer and published them in this book. To balance things, I've included research from a selection of numerous

Beatles biographies, sprinkled with research about life in the sixties, and supplemented by comments made by individuals, like me, who got on board for our own Magical Mystery Tour.

This is, by no means, a definitive Beatles biography. Rather it is a biographical sketch of one devoted fan whose life was enriched by four souls she may, or may not, have known in a prior lifetime.

Chapter One

The Sixties, the Beatles, and the Catholic Church

I don't recall any fanfare when the calendar slipped from 1959 to 1960, but there was just something about the date that felt a bit disconcerting, even to a child. Little did I know how much would be packed into that decade or how deeply my life would be impacted by the transformational seeds that were being planted in an entire generation.

In his book, *The Spiritual Meaning of the Sixties*, Tobias Churton expresses a similar sentiment: "There are many people today who believe that there was something peculiarly special about the Sixties, not just in sociological and political terms, not only in the technical fields of lunar exploration, cinema, and music . . . but in the spiritual dimension. Something, it is believed by believers, was *going on.*" He goes on to say that the "youth movements of the time were also undergoing a spiritual crisis."

From an astrological perspective, Eric Meyers states that "the 1960s emphasized the process of spiritual awakening" but that wasn't something I had any inkling of as I lived my day-to-day life in the Chicago southside neighborhood of Bridgeport.

Although today Bridgeport is one of Chicago's most diverse neighborhoods, in the sixties it was a segregated community that had, as we liked to say, a church on one corner and a tavern on the other. Life seemed to circulate around both, with the men favoring the taverns while the families, usually led by the women, designed their lives around the church. The Catholic Church did not accept reincarnation as a reality. During the twelve years I attended Catholic school, none of the nuns, priests or lay teachers ever raised the topic, much less encouraged private exploration of this eastern philosophy. If I raised a question about reincarnation, I would be chastised with: "Don't you know the Catholic Church is the one true church?" My peers did not entertain the idea that reincarnation was real, and yet, as a teenager, that's all I thought about. Perhaps it was the Beatles who gave me license to do that.

Candy Leonard captures how other Catholic girls were feeling at that time. She quotes a female fan as saying: "I didn't like Catholic school, I felt misunderstood, and I felt restricted, especially as a girl. The Beatles made me realize that if I could just stick it out, there was something bigger out there."

Leonard goes on to say: "From the beginning, they [the Beatles] told these young people it was okay to be reflective and to think about big ideas. Through their songs and their own high-profile adventures, they encouraged fans to question and quest. Several fans said, 'They made us think about things in different ways.'"

Considering my confrontations with the clergy at St. Anthony de Padua and later at St. Barbara High School, I'd say that was more than true. Even when I was still playing with Barbies, I had this gnawing feeling that there had to be more to my relationship with God than what they were pedaling at the parochial schools. I felt a heaviness, as if there wasn't much more to life than this darkness I experienced at every turn. Nothing made sense and it felt rather hopeless to even dream otherwise.

I did not consider jumping to another religion at that time. I was too young to make that choice on my own, and I was too fearful to do it until I was much, much older. Embracing Hinduism never entered my mind. Yet years later, George Harrison expressed his conclusion about the two in a very succinct way.

"I believe much more in the religions of India than in anything I ever learned from Christianity," Joshua Greene quotes him as saying. "The difference over here is that their religion is every second and every minute of their lives."

The Catholic Church did little to bring spirituality into their teachings. We learned how to be good Catholic girls and boys. We could recite the names of every part of the priest's vestment and each item on the altar, but if we experienced a crisis of any kind, we did not know how to have a personal relationship with God wherein we would find solace. For those of us who were yearning to find something of meaning outside of ourselves, there were no tools at our disposal to tap into that divine wisdom that we held within. Heck—the whole idea of holding divine wisdom within one's soul was a foreign idea in most traditional churches.

Every week, my class was marched over to the church adjacent to our school so we could confess our sins. I sat in the pew awaiting my turn to be forced into confessing sins I either did not commit, or were so trivial as not worth mentioning. How many times did I disobey my parents for God's sake? But we had to confess something, so I'd sit in the pew and review the pamphlet provided to us that had all the sins one could confess listed there for our convenience. How often did my mind wander into my obsessive thoughts about the soul, i.e., what was it really? How did it operate? What did it look like? Where was it kept? Was it eternal in the sense of inhabiting multiple bodies over time? I would stare at the statues and stained glass, hoping an answer would come to me, but it never did, and I knew the church would never address this in a manner that satisfied my hunger for deeper meaning. On and on, I felt as though I was held captive in a fog that robbed me of any sense of higher meaning or fulfillment.

As I read more esoteric books, the theory of karma began making a lot more sense than sin. Karma—the philosophy of reap what you sow—meant there was a just and divine source overseeing things. With this philosophy, you couldn't get a clean slate just by going to confession.

Somewhere, somehow, you would have to answer for your thoughts, words, and deeds. With karma, it made sense why there were some who were poor versus rich; healthy versus ill; successful versus failing; some living to a ripe old age and others dying so young; and on and on it went. Every facet of life, when applied to karma, made perfect sense. And when I thought about it, living a life under the self-responsibility eye of karma was considerably more difficult than worrying about a mortal sin that I could easily get erased by confessing it to a priest—God's so-called agent on Earth.

As Churton wrote about this time: "There was some awareness that there *was* something to reach for, something out there, or rather, in *here*. Somewhere. Something."

Even John Lennon echoed that sentiment. Barry Miles, writing in *Beatles In Their Own Words*, quotes John as saying: "There's something else to life, isn't there? This isn't it, surely?"

I don't think anyone in my generation realized this restlessness was happening on a global scale. In *The Cynical Idealist: The Spiritual Biography of John Lennon*, Gary Tillery writes that by the mid-1960s, baby boomers were maturing and assuming idealistic values:

> The self-reinforcing energy of the "youthquake" led to widespread speculation and belief that a new stage of consciousness was developing, a leap forward by the species, with the Western

nations leading the way—a transformation that would coincide with the supposed dawning of the Age of Aquarius.[1]

Certainly, the very nature of what was happening in the sixties played a role in our evolutionary process. Christopher Hill, writing in *Into The Mystic: The Visionary and Ecstatic Roots of 1960s Rock and Roll,* considers some of the themes of 1960s rock and roll. "Among these, first and foremost," he writes, "is the fascination with alterations of consciousness, ecstatic states, mystical experience, and gnosis, as well as a sense of wonder and the numinous . . . There is a strong interest in the exotic, in Eastern spiritual traditions, in myth and archaic wisdom, in the primitive and primal."

In *Blackbird: The Life and Times of Paul McCartney*, Geoffrey Giuliano writes: "Unlike the youth of today, who seem intent on using drugs to numb themselves to the reality of life around them, the youth of the sixties considered dropping acid as a key to inner knowledge and heightened self-awareness." That may have been true for many of my contemporaries, but for the most part, the Beatle fans I was around did not talk about that, much less address the concept of achieving self-awareness on any level.

I never understood why my very strict, conservative parents allowed me to take over the basement to turn it into a fan club and then maintain it for the next eight years. The answer may be contained in something George

Martin wrote: "That enjoyable charisma came through to the world at large, which was seeing something it had not seen before. It was an expression of youth, a slight kicking-over of the traces, which found a ready response in young people. Curiously, it was a response that the parents, though they might not have liked the music themselves, did not seem to begrudge." For my parents, my listening to Beatles music, having friends over and running a fan club, was the lesser of two evils when you considered what was going on with some of my peers and their sexual and drug exploration.

For George, the use of drugs supplemented what he was already experiencing. Graeme Thomson writes: "He read the *Yoga Sutras*, where he heard echoes of the same revelation he'd had the first time he took acid: the soul was infinite, and though it was the size of 'one-thousandth part of the tip of a hair,' it had the power of 'ten thousand suns.'"

Still, as Christopher Hill writes, the door to attaining that level of awareness was all around us: "The work of the sixties musicians was intended, like Hindu mandalas or Eastern Orthodox icons, to set as a trigger to transmit a new way of seeing," later adding that rock and roll music was not just the soundtrack of our teenage lives, but was also "playing some mysterious but significant part in a transformation that was coming over the Western world, if not the globe."

Across the ocean, a future Beatle was experiencing the same thing. Religion was not of importance to George's father, so as a child George went to Catholic services with his mother until he made his first Holy Communion. That was as far as he went.

Writing in *The Lyrics*, Paul discusses his family's attitude toward religion: "I just naturally grew up thinking that the right thing was to be tolerant, the right thing was to be good. We were never told at home that you shalt *not* do this, you shalt *not* do that."

In another comment written in *The Lyrics*, Paul said: "I do believe in the idea that there is some sort of higher force that can help us."

One cannot discuss the sixties without bringing to mind that tragic day, November 22, 1963, when President John F. Kennedy was assassinated. If anything represented the epitome of the darkness, this was it. His death was a watershed moment in my life and the lives of many around me. We were changed forever. Even though I was young when Kennedy was in office, there was something about his administration and his family that let a sliver of light into our lives. When he died, I cried openly, which was uncharacteristic of me. My mother was appalled, saying I expressed more emotion at Kennedy's death than I did at the death of close relatives. That's true. But what she didn't understand was that those tears were shed for an entirely different reason, and that black cloud that was always following me had grown darker and consumed every aspect of my being. I was thirteen with my whole life in front of me, and yet I felt despondent, unable to enjoy life because on some deep level I knew that a serious shift had occurred, and not toward the light but away from it. I wasn't the only one who felt that way, but I did not have the wherewithal at that age to know how to seek out others who shared my yearning for the light.

That is, until the Beatles. They didn't know it—and neither did we—but they would become, as Churton suggests, symbols of change and anchor a new phase in human consciousness.

The Beatles arrived in America just a few months after Kennedy's assassination. Writing about their impact at that particular time in history, Paul says: "…though it's not for me to say, people have written that the country, especially teenagers, had been looking for something new and positive and fun to latch onto after mourning his death. It's one possible explanation for why Beatlemania took off so quickly in the U.S."

We weren't the only ones who were thinking about things in different ways during the height of Beatlemania. Our discontent was shared with George Harrison who said: "Turning to churches to find Jesus or temples to find God meant searching in the wrong places. Each person had but to look within."

Gary Tillery writes: ". . . Harrison viewed Jesus as a fully realized incarnation of God who deserved reverence. The poor carpenter from Galilee had come to understand the great secret, burned out his karma, and manifested the deity within himself."[2]

George believed that everything seekers were yearning for was not outside themselves, but within. But that wasn't a concept that Beatles fans even considered in those early years. Nonetheless, the discontent led to exploring alternatives to Christian philosophies. That was certainly the case with me.

As I thought about it, I realized the pump had been primed long before the Beatles came around. During my teenage years, when they were at the peak of their popularity, I began to openly question Catholicism and seek answers about life and death that were not forthcoming in my religion classes at school or the sermons on Sunday. So much of what I was taught as a young Catholic student never made sense to me. I remember when I was seven—the age of reason when you knew enough about right and wrong to be responsible for your actions and therefore started accumulating sins—I was haunted by this one question: If I forgot it was Friday and went home and had a ham sandwich for lunch, then got struck by a car in the crosswalk heading back to school and died, I'd end up in hell? After all, eating meat on Friday was a mortal sin back then and, in that circumstance, I wouldn't have time to rush to the confessional before my soul left my body. Is this what a just and loving Creator would do to a little kid?

Years later, another equally disturbing scenario had me asking the same questions. When I was twelve, my friends and I went to see the movie, *Gypsy*, starring Natalie Wood. According to the church, that was a "B" rated movie, which meant it was not approved for someone my age. When the nuns discovered a group of us saw the film, they sent us to confess our terrible transgression to our parish pastor, Father Randolph. I'll never forget what he said: "You wouldn't deliberately run into a house that was on fire, would you?" I asked myself, what did that have to do with seeing a movie about a stripper? Oh—I get it. Just seeing it was the equivalent of a fiery doom because if I died leaving the matinee, I'd go straight to the depths of hell. Oh Lord. How do I get out of this one? I'll kneel at the altar, say my penance of ten Our Father's and ten Hail Mary's, which Father Randolph said would be sufficient in this case, and then I would get to walk out of the church squeaky clean again.

The whole thing was absurd. I kept asking myself if what we were being taught was truly representative of what Jesus would do? No matter how I tried to spin it, the answer was no. Something wasn't right, but I didn't know what it was. There had to be another answer to how the universe doled out justice. Clearly the cycle of sin-confession-sin-confession wasn't it. But what was?

This took place during the pre-Beatles era, so at that time, and actually even after the Beatles surfaced, I did not pay attention to what religion John, Paul, George or Ringo grew up in. What I later learned, however, that like me, George was expressing a lot of doubt. Joshua M. Greene writes that religion made no sense to George. George told photographer Murray Silver he was raised Catholic but even as a child he couldn't understand why Jesus was proclaimed to be the only Son of God. George believed we were all sons and daughters of God.

Author David Bennahum quotes George from two different interviews, addressing the issue of God and the church:

> It is one of our perennial problems, whether there is a God. From the Hindu point of view each soul is divine. All religions are branches of one big tree . . . The thing is, you go to an ordinary church and it's a nice feeling. They all tell you about God, but they don't show you the way. They don't show you how to become Christ-conscious yourself. Hinduism is different.

A similar sentiment is expressed by Nicholas Schaffner in *The Beatles Forever*: "At a time when the last vestiges of traditional Western belief were being discarded by growing numbers of disoriented young people, they were particularly susceptible to any sage (or charlatan) who seemed to offer a convincing replacement." This was life in the sixties. Churton writes:

> . . . Unfortunately, longstanding suspicion and rejection of mysticism in the churches bore its fruit in indifference to the spiritual meaning and experience, and were, perforce, driven outside of the churches in search of it. If, as the churches

believe, they did in fact possess the whole store of spiritual meaning for humankind, then they demonstrated a woeful inability to express or understand this possession meaningfully, or make common cause with other opponents of materialism ... The movement away from established religion toward the personal quest is undoubtedly a key aspect of the spiritual meaning of the Sixties, and did we understand the matter better as a culture, would be cause for some celebration and confidence.

Gary Tillery states that George:

... was especially disturbed that so many people appeared more preoccupied with the trappings of religion than with its spiritual value ... He felt that religion was "all screwed up" because it seemed to have no heart—that it ought to be about how people treated other people and what they gave to others, not what they received as believers.[3]

According to Ray Comfort, writing in *The Beatles, God & The Bible*, while touring Britain in October 1964, Paul told *Playboy*, "None of us believe in God." Comfort goes on to write that John later adjusted his statement to say that they were agnostic, not necessarily atheist.

In Tillery's book on John Lennon, he makes it clear that John did not associate himself with any religion: "With the exception of his brief association with the Maharishi Mahesh Yogi, Lennon never exhibited a desire to belong to a larger spiritual group."[4] John, it seemed, had an aversion to labels and insisted he did not belong to anything, much less an organized religion.

Of course, fans had no idea that any of the Beatles were giving serious thought to spiritual evolution. It eventually became obvious with George, but lesser so with the others. I certainly had no idea that John was on a spiritual search. Fans knew early on that John was an independent thinker, and that often intimidated us—at least, it did me. But we had few clues to say his thinking encompassed a more spiritual meaning to life. The one thing we did agree on was that we were rejecting the beliefs handed down to us. Like John, we wanted to find our own way, but we did not have the tools nor the mentors to show us how.

We certainly did not know that one night in 1966 John prayed for guidance to address the meaninglessness he felt. We had no idea he felt that way, and yet, that night began what according to Gary Tillery, was "the beginning of a search lasting for a decade, an anguished search for an alternative foundation on which Lennon could orient his life."[5] To do that, Tillery said John began to study the works of Sigmund Freud, C.G. Jung, and Wilhelm Reich. Those names would reverberate throughout my own later studies of metaphysics. So many catalysts for change were acting independently of each other in the sixties and yet they were all connected—each playing their own significant role in the evolution of an entire generation.

Chapter Two

1964-5: Fixing a Hole

1964

On February 7, 1964, the Fab Four descended from the heavens. Actually, they alit from a Pan Am Yankee Clipper Flight 101 from London Heathrow Airport that landed at New York's Kennedy Airport. There they were. Barely off the plane, waving at the 3,000 screaming teenage fans—girls my age, for goodness sake. Why were those girls screaming like that? What did they know that I didn't? So okay, these English guys were cute, but what was causing all this mass hysteria?

I made note of the date and it's a good thing I did. Everyone has watershed dates in their life; those unexpected days when something extraordinary happens and your life shifts from one direction to another. February 7, 1964 was one of those dates for me and countless others. But how could I have possibly known on that Friday, as I watched television in the five-room flat I shared with my parents and brother, that it would turn out to be one of the most pivotal days of my life?

From an early age, I kept a diary. It may have been a subconscious remnant of prior lifetimes in which I made it a habit to record the events of the day so I would have something to refer to if needed in the future. Curiously, the first mention of the Beatles in my diary does not happen until February 12, three days after they made their first appearance on *The Ed Sullivan Show*. I was one of 73 million lucky viewers in the United States to watch that television performance. I don't remember what I was thinking between their TV premiere and the mention of their name for the first time in my diary, but it must have been significant. I wrote that I went to my friend Dorine's house on the 12th and according to my diary, we started talking about the Beatles and how cute they were. Little did I know this would be the start of an odyssey that would last for the next eight years and then continue to influence me for decades after the Beatles were no more.

It also would be the start of synchronistic events in my young life that would propel me deeper into Beatlemania, more as an active player than a devoted fan. In looking back for whatever clues I could find on how the Beatles became such a major influence in my life, I discovered many unforeseen family events that contributed to that outcome. Two days after I made my first Beatles-related diary entry, my paternal grandmother died. It was Valentine's Day, and my diary only mentions the turmoil in my family and my fear that I would lose all contact with my closest cousin. My paternal grandfather had died six months earlier and the circumstances of his death sparked a rift between my father and his sister. My aunt had three children, and my brother and I had a sibling-like relationship with the youngest two—a boy and girl close to our age. My grandfather's death had escalated the family tension in true Sicilian fashion, but as long as my grandmother was alive, the door remained open for the hope of reconciliation.

When she died, I feared it would trigger a final split in the family. Unfortunately, that's exactly what happened. Perhaps it was fortuitous that the Beatles came into my life when they did, filling the painful void left by my father's estrangement from his family and the subsequent loss of access to our beloved cousins. We were cut off without warning and without so much as a goodbye. Attempts on our part to reach them by mail were met with silence. Our hearts were broken on such a profound level, that even well into adulthood we still recall the pain of that separation.

As a grieving fourteen-year-old, I sought solace in reading and music. But where the Beatles were concerned, I wanted more than to be a silent observer. I sensed I had natural leadership skills that I had not fully embraced. I also knew I was a fairly good writer and organizer. All I needed was to find a cause that would be so all-consuming I wouldn't have time to grieve; something where I not only could utilize those skills, but in doing so, somehow make my mark and find some semblance of joy. And that brought me back to the Beatles. It wasn't much of a stretch to me to realize that forming a Beatles Fan Club was the answer.

Our basement was the perfect place to run the club. With a private backdoor entrance, my friends could come and go without disturbing my parents. It didn't take long for me to transform that dull space into a Beatle fan's paradise. I plastered the walls with every Beatle picture I could find from *Tiger Beat* and the myriad other teen magazines that were published in the 1960s. In no time, the knotty-pine walls became invisible beneath the posters of "the lads."

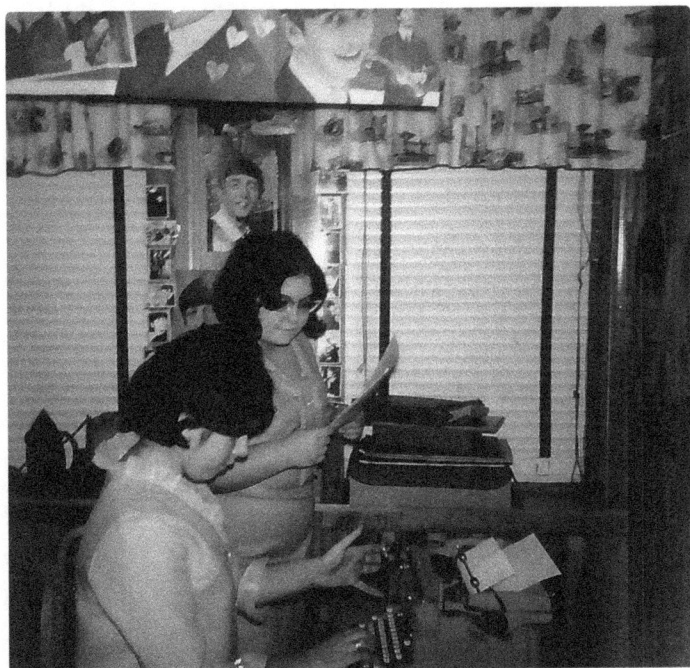

I turned an old kitchen table into my desk and I put my mom's clunky Underwood typewriter next to it so I could swing around to type my letters and membership materials. I gathered up as many office supplies I could find and I brought my stereo downstairs so I could listen to music while I worked. In no time I was open for business.

In discussing the unseen benefit of this work, Christine Feldman–Barrett writes: "Some fans would later acknowledge that their Beatles fandom launched, shaped, or greatly informed their careers."

This was certainly the case with me. I did not know it then, but those years I spent running the club enabled me to hone in on talents, skills and abilities I would later use. My three by five index card system, for instance, would morph into a database. My collection of magazines and newspapers, searching for stories, would enhance my research skills. My monthly newsletter would sharpen my writing and production skills. My copying, printing and selling photographs would teach me something about being an entrepreneur. My experience working with downtown hotels to reserve meeting space would be utilized years later when I became a trade show coordinator for a telecommunications company, and then when I organized meetings, large-scale lectures and conferences for myself and for the A.R.E. My constant typing away at my mother's Underwood did wonders for increasing my accuracy and speed. By the time I was in high school, I could type considerably faster than my peers and won an award for that ability in both my junior and senior years.

The work I did on behalf of the Beatles was strictly voluntary. While it was very much "a job," I took no salary, nor did I expect to earn any money. Anything I did make, via the sales of products, went right back into the club. It seemed to me we were always in the red, as evidenced by my constant pleas for members to pay their dues on time. According to Christine Feldman Barrett:

> Most female fans who sought Beatles-related work in the 1960s—many of whom were teen-agers—became local branch secretaries for the

Official Beatles Fan Club. While these positions were clerical and, therefore, traditionally "feminine," they also offered girls a sense of fun and sociality while also developing various skills and competencies. It is not difficult to imagine the heightened sense of responsibility these teenagers must have felt by involving themselves in an enterprise promoting one of the biggest cultural phenomena in the world. Doing something purposeful for the Beatles also helped these girls carve out a distinct identity for themselves. According to a 1964 interview with the Australian teens who ran Sydney's Beatles Fan Club, they were no longer the "normal girls" they had been prior to taking on this work. Instead, they were organizing meaningful events and experiences for their local community. Even more importantly, and often only understood retrospectively by the women in question— "working for the Beatles" sometimes allowed young women to catch a glimpse of future careers.

In terms of my future careers—the type of careers that actually gave me a paycheck—I can see how my work as a fan club president, greatly enhanced my capabilities. What it didn't do was enhance my common sense when it came to the type of jobs I accepted. Nearly all of them were secretarial jobs that became demoralizing experiences.

One in particular was such an abusive environment that I developed colitis. I left and got a job in the advertising department of a telecommunications company closer to home. I started as an office manager, but once I learned our department was responsible for the printed sales material for the product line, and for an employee newsletter, I asked if I could try my hand at copywriting. They agreed and I moved up the ranks to copywriter and trade show coordinator.

This job, like my previous job, produced an even higher level of stress and after a few years, I left to work for a company that built and ran apartment buildings and a health club/restaurant/hotel chain. I came in to start their advertising and public relations department, and I did that well. However, like the previous company, this was a predominantly male business, and I often was treated like the Christian in the lion's den.

After the birth of my first child, I left the corporate world and began a freelance writing career. I wrote profiles of local business owners for *The Daily Herald*, and later wrote advertising copy for Dominick's, a much-loved food store chain in the Chicago area. But it was my working with my friend David Johnson, a graphic designer I met when we both worked at that telecommunications company, that turned out to be most fortuitous. David had started his own graphic design business and occasionally needed a copywriter. He asked if I was interested in providing copy for some of his projects and I jumped at the chance to work with him again.

One of David's most charismatic clients was a man I'll refer to as Simon, who was a medical hypnoanalyst. He hired David to design brochures to cover various aspects of his practice, especially in the area of weight loss and smoking cessation. I was brought in to write the copy, so I would attend meetings with Simon and his assistant, Pam, in order to get a feel for what they were doing. It was during these meetings that I learned that Simon did past-life regressions. When I confided to Pam my interest in this area, and also my ability to do Soul Writing, she and Simon became fascinated by what I could do for them in that regard. Simon was open to exploring all aspects of metaphysical topics. He even hosted a cable television program in which he interviewed a variety of individuals involved in esoteric studies. One of them was a channeler who would play an important role in the past-life organization I would start years later.

Simon insisted that the only way I could write about his hypnosis technique was for me to experience it myself, so I began a series of sessions in his office as if I were a client. This was an eye-opening experience for me in that it not only introduced me first-hand to hypnosis, but to past-life exploration and channeling.

At one point, Simon suggested we form our own past-life organization he called MAPLE, Midwest Association for Past-Life Exploration. I began doing publicity for it, had several feature articles published in local newspapers, and started hosting programs with Simon as our speaker. When he was interviewed on a Chicago radio station, he mentioned MAPLE, giving the organization a huge boost in interest. I was excited about being a part of MAPLE, but it ended badly and Simon and I parted company. Shortly after that, I formed PLEXUS.

In thinking about my work history in general, I learned something about myself that I wished I knew sooner. I was much happier when I worked for myself. I always thought of myself as a team player, but in reality, I was better off when I was the captain of my own ship. Just as with the Beatles fan club when I was running it on my own, whenever I tried to bring in others to take on some of the responsibility, it never worked. There was always conflict, and I found whatever progress I made on my own began to slip whenever I watered it down with someone else's energy. This pattern would continue for years. It's a lesson I only recently identified. The work I do now is singular in nature, and I'm all the happier for it, even though I learned it in the school of hard knocks.

Running a Beatles fan club had its ups and downs, too. In terms of incentives, Feldman-Barret writes:

> Though the possibility of meeting the Beatles incentivized girls to take on these projects and positions, there were other important benefits. Significantly, within these roles, Beatlemaniacs

were not ridiculed or belittled. These teenagers' efforts were valued by adult professionals who saw them as integral players within a newly popular (and profitable) youth culture phenomenon. The same girls who were sometimes disparaged in mainstream press accounts as immature "screamers" were taking on challenges and responsibilities that demonstrated maturity, resilience, and grit. Their fandom may have given them a clear "mission" (meeting the Beatles) but it also helped them realize their own capabilities. Much to their credit, they fearlessly interacted with other high-profile, adult professionals . . . While it must have occurred to these young women that transforming Beatlemania into a type of part-time job was somewhat unusual, this awareness fortified rather than inhibited their efforts. Moreover, the goals they set and the chances they took only served to bolster their sense of self.

I'd like to state for the record that the possibility of meeting the Beatles was something I never seriously entertained. You may think that odd, considering my passionate involvement in running a Beatles fan club, but in truth, I was far too insecure to put myself in a position of actually meeting them. Instead, I saw myself more as the "behind the scenes" person. I was awestruck, but at the same time, I cringed when I learned of fans going to London to track down one or more of the Beatles at their homes or recording studio. I never understood how they had the nerve to do that. It seemed like such a pretentious thing to do—to literally show up at their door or ambush them on the sidewalk. Have you no self-respect? But that was my issue—not theirs. So fearful was I of how I'd feel emotionally if I was the one out on the sidewalk, only to be ignored or worse—snubbed—that I never went to England, nor did I seek them out after a local concert. I never even wrote them a fan letter. Interestingly, while I went out of my way to not be noticed, events in the fan club some years later would thrust me into the spotlight.

The club I started in 1964 would take on many incarnations over the next eight years. It began as a more generic club called *The Society for the Prevention of Cruelty to the Beatles.* I don't remember the logic of choosing this name, and I wish I had been more creative than that, but there you have it.

Far cleverer, if I do say so myself, was the name of the club's very first newsletter, *The Beatles Bugle*, which I published in April 1964. The entire issue acted as a primer for new Beatle fans, providing "some of the facts that every Beatle fan should know about those fab Beatles."

Without computers or graphic design programs, I did the best I could with the primitive tools at my disposal. Not happy with my initial creation, the following month I changed the look of the newsletter, having studied the

page 2

The Society For the Prevention Of Cruelty to the Beatles

BEATLES FOREVER   APR -- 1964

Dear Member,

Here are some of the facts that every Beatle fan should know about these fab Beatles.

James Paul McCartney
Age: 21
Born: June 18, 1942
Height: 5 feet 11 inches
Eyes: Dark brown
Hair: Black
Likes: sweaters, music, reading,
writing songs with John Lennon,
fooling around with Ringo's drums,
and likes any type of girl except
a soft one.

Paul came from the small town of
Allerton, a suburb just outside
Liverpool, England. When he was a
little boy he was very interested
in art. He used to sit home nights
waiting for his mother to come home,
while his father used to... in the
kitchen preparing supper, and Paul
sitting there with a pen and a piece
of paper in his hand, his father
being a salesman, didn't bring home
enough money to support them, so his
mother had to be a nurse and had to work very hard. She died when he was
only fourteen years old. When he was about fifteen years old he got
interested in music. He used to wander around the streets looking for places
to listen to the music he loved. He used to wander over to the cafes and there
he met John Lennon who was also interested in music. This was the beginning
of the fabulous Beatles. Now he and John write all the songs for the group
and have turned in over a hundred tunes since, which have all become hits.
Paul is known as the nut Beatle or the Beatle nut. He is the zaniest of the
lot, the quietest wit, the sharpest tongue, and the loudest laugh, the wackiest
imagination and a crazy sense of humor. As you can see Paul is really fab.

PAUL

P is for the pleading voice of yours that sends us in a daze,
A is for the bank account you have from what each week pays,
U is for the ugliness that you don't seem to own,
L is for the love we could give every night when you come home.

John Winston Lennon
Age: 23
Born: October 9, 1940
Height: 5 feet 11 inches
Eyes: brown
Hair: brown
Likes: the color black, music,
books, painting, television,
modern jazz, leather, and
suede nightwear.

John's mother died before his four-
teenth birthday. He then went to live
with his aunt Mimi. He was brought up
in the heart of Liverpool. He went to
Dovedale Primary School and Quarry Bank
Grammar School. And then on to Liverpool
College of Art. Art was always his best
subject at school but he failed miserably
at his science and wasn't too hot
in history. When he went to Dovedale,
he knew George Harrison by sight, but
because of age difference of nearly three years they didn't get to know each
other. He met Paul McCartney several years later as they taught each other how
to play the guitar. They practiced very hard at it, when they thought that they
were good enough they went for and additional calling themselves the Nurk Twins.
They got accepted and they were booked for a spot. A few years later they met
George and the Beatles were on their way. They went to Germany to do a show.
George and Paul were interested in the girls but not John, because his girl
was at home.

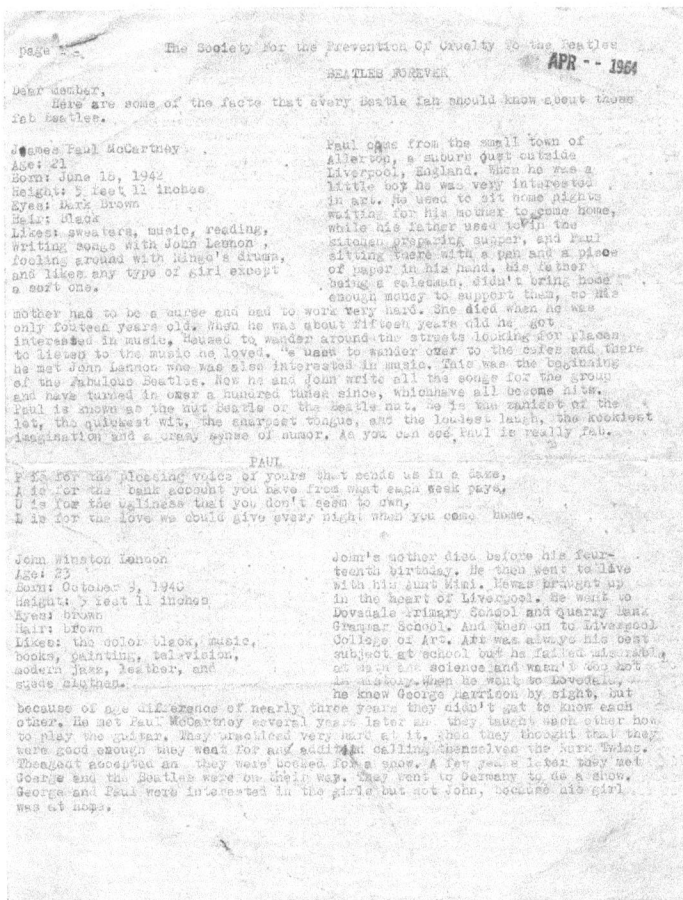

format of magazines I found around the house. I convinced three of my friends to join the newsletter's staff, naming myself as editor and my friends as columnists. The hot tidbits that month were that Ringo was engaged and the Russians were claiming to have had the Beatles first.

The three-page newsletter was done on white onionskin paper with a line down the middle to separate columns.

BEATLES BUGLE

MAY EDITION (64)

WRITERS

EDITOR - JOANNE MAGGIO

JOKES - TINA CONTINO

BEATLES - DORINE JIRKA

CLUB NEWS - DORINE & JOANNE

BEATLES FRANDS - DORINE

GEORGE - DORINE JIRKA

RINGO - JOANNE MAGGIO

JOHN - MARGIE BULANDA

PAUL - MARGIE BULANDA

OTHERS - JOANNE MAGGIO

BEATLES NEWS

by DORINE

Beatle fans, it is so hard to keep up on our Beatles. So I will try to do my best on finding out information for you.

I would appreciate it if you would give me bits of information to help me along.

At last count, I heard that Beatles John and George are enjoying themselves in Honolulu and Ringo and Paul are in the Virgin Islands and have two young ladies with them.

There is a rumor going around that Ringo is engaged. Don't believe it. He is neither engaged or has any intention of getting engaged.

The song, Do you want to know a Secret is supposed to be sung by Beatle George, at least that is what they say. I don't believe it and I don't think that you should believe it either. If you listen closely, you would hear that it is John's voice and only John's voice.

The Russians claim that they had the Beatles first. They said that they had a group like the Beatles before the Beatles came about. Of course you and I know that it isn't true so we won't discuss it any further now.

In the London zoo there are two cubs named after George and Ringo so we are happy about that.

Club member Margie Bulanda has a friend that just got back from London. She says they have nothing about the Beatles out there, but all the boys have Beatle haircuts.

On WYNR they had a contest between the Beatles and red hot rythem and blues. The Beatles won of course.

Another of the rumors that are going around is that John's wife Cynthia is going to have another baby. It could be true but I doubt it. CONTINUED

Each column's headlines were hand-printed in black magic marker, and the text was individually typed. Although I was a fairly good typist, I was by no means a perfectionist, and I am embarrassed to admit, made little attempt to correct my typos. By today's standards, it was abominable, but considering it was done on a manual typewriter in those years before word processors were invented, it adequately served its purpose.

As editor, I knew enough to make sure there was a variety of information in the newsletter. We featured "Beatle stories"—a short paragraph on each Beatle and what they were up to. Paul was declared the most "beautiful" Beatle and the author of that article gave him the nickname "Bouncy." The writer of the George article said, "I guess he is the kind of guy that could make someone happy." For the piece on John, the author suggested we would all die if we didn't have John's music, saying she believed John—and not Paul—was responsible for most of their songs and added they were dedicated to Cynthia. She believed that, but looking back, we all know that was just wishful thinking. She continued: "You know that John loves Cynthia above all other things and always has her on his mind." Right. I wrote a short piece on Ringo, debating the issue of whether he was the sexy Beatle—as if I knew anything about sex. I vowed he was the one I wanted and would get, even if it took an eternity." Dream on, Jo Jo.

What I find so astonishing now, some sixty years later, is that there are Beatles groups on Facebook that sound a lot like we did in '64! That same level of immature naivete is alive and well; perhaps more a natural rite of passage than I realized.

In producing my newsletters, I took advantage of my position as editor to ascend a soapbox and produce a column called "Comments." In the introductory piece, I wrote that I hoped that newsletter wouldn't be the last, as if I was already anticipating on some subliminal level that I needed to enjoy the present moment because it would not last for long. I had no idea that I'd continue to publish a Beatles newsletter, in various "incarnations" for eight years until my farewell issue in January 1972—not a bad run for an amateur.

In many ways, the newsletters were chronicling my own evolution. Reading between the lines of my editorials, it's apparent to me now that I was trying to work out the enormous conflict created by my family's drama. On the one hand, I was enjoying the high that any devoted fan feels when you are deriving pleasure from being involved with someone you admire. On the other hand, I was running a fan club where I had to contend with many diverse personalities. I had neither the experience nor the emotional maturity to do either and that disparity was reflected in my writing.

The year 1964 had many pivotal events, including the signing of The Civil Rights Act into law. Profound changes were happening on a global scale, and unbeknown to us who knew nothing about astrology, changes were happening on an astrological scale as well. According to Eric Meyers:

> 1964 featured a major planetary shift. The planet Saturn is the dominant energy of the cultural milieu. It was completing its passage through the sign of new trends and fascination, modernizing

culture. The proliferation of rock music led by electric guitars and authentic self-expression was fitting. On March 24th, it began a passage of deeper subtlety, imagery and inspiration. For the next 2.5 to 3 years, the emphasis was on spirituality, which the Beatles would progressively develop throughout the passage.

Two important Beatles-related events also occurred in 1964. The first was the release of the Beatles first feature film, *A Hard Day's Night*, which came out in July. I saw it thirteen times when it was first released. In those days, you could go to the theater and stay to watch a film over and over again. The film has been hailed as "the greatest rock-and-roll comedy adventure ever," but Beatle fans didn't sit there and think about the film's plot as much as they salivated at seeing the objects of their affection up close on the silver screen, even if they were in black and white. It was in this film that we were introduced to Pattie Boyd, the beautiful blonde model who had a small role in the film and would go on to marry George two years later.

The other significant event came on September 5, 1964, when the Beatles gave their first concert in Chicago at the International Amphitheatre. This was the same indoor arena that four years later would make national news as the location of the anti-war riots during the 1968 Democratic National Convention. The Amphitheatre, located on 43rd & Halsted, was a Bridgeport landmark and was less than two miles from my house. It may as well have been two-thousand miles because I was one of the devastated fans who were unable to secure tickets to the concert. I consoled myself by saying "there will be a next time."

1965

The Civil Rights movement dominated the news in 1965. Race riots broke out in the Watts neighborhood of Los Angeles, California. The Voting Rights Act became law. Dr. Martin Luther King Jr. led the civil rights march from Selma to Montgomery, Alabama. Malcom X was shot in New York. While those of us wrapped up in the Beatles were aware of these historic events happening all around us, many of us were either too young or too focused on the Beatles and their music to truly absorb the importance of the events we were living through. It's hard to believe the two were happening simultaneously and depending on where your consciousness led you, individuals were having very different experiences of what it meant to be alive in 1965.

On a more subliminal level, I sense that 1965 marked the earliest inkling of spiritual seeds being planted by the Beatles. As an example, author Candy Leonard writes about the impact of the song, "The Word," which appeared on the *Rubber Soul* album: "A year and a half before the 'Summer of Love' and their 1967 anthem 'All You Need is Love,' the Beatles were advocating love as a universal principle, and, quite explicitly, positioning themselves as the spiritual leaders of the emerging youth movement and counterculture, announcing they are 'here to show everybody the light.'"

Of course, I did not see it that way—yet. I was more absorbed in the day-to-day operations of running a fan club. By January, the *Beatles Bugle* had grown to ten pages, but my feeling of success at having grown the newsletter did not make up for a difficult year in which I had lost two of my closest cousins—one because of the aforementioned family feud, and another who moved to California. I was feeling abandoned and desperately alone. As if my problems with my family weren't bad enough, I was having ongoing issues with my friends, especially those who were helping me with the fan club. Most were doing it begrudgingly. I found myself resorting to bribery to keep them involved, offering them more columns to write or a fancy title to placate their egos and keep them on board.

My first editorial in that issue reflected that struggle and offered the first evidence of a behavior pattern I would take into my later metaphysical career. More and more, I used my position as editor as a soapbox. Back then, I reasoned that since I was doing all the work and was responsible for the club, that I could pontificate on whatever topic I chose. When I was doing research for this book, I reread that January 1965 editorial. Revisiting it from the standpoint of who I am today, my attention became riveted on the third paragraph in which the theme of "family" began to emerge.

"Now that we are starting a new year," I wrote, "let's become a family. A family for the Beatles. Don't let ANY-ONE or ANYTHING throw the Beatles from the top. That is, you have to see to it that you stay a Beatlemaniac from dawn to dusk. That is what I have been since last February and believe me, I have never been happier or have had more fun since they came into my life. They have shown me exactly what a wonderful feeling is and what the friendship of fellow Beatlemaniacs who share your goal can mean."

But I wasn't happy, and I certainly wasn't having fun. What I was really saying was: "My own family has abandoned me—don't you abandon me, too." Clearly, all I wanted was to "fix a hole."

In the coming years, I'd use the analogy of family often—that we were a "family for the Beatles." Whether other Beatle fans shared this sentiment, I don't know. What I know now is that it was just more evidence of my need to be among like-minded people who shared my beliefs, my passion, and my desire to give of myself to what I believed in. To this day, I use the terms "like-minded" and "soul family" in my writings. In revisiting my 1965 Beatles newsletters, this is clearly where it originated.

At fourteen, I may have been verbalizing how important it was for me to identify with people who were like me because I had no experience working with a diversified populace. My neighborhood, my church, my school, and my family offered little, if any, diversification whatsoever.

So for me, finding folks who believed what I believed, who looked like me, who had the same interests, felt important. You would think that my family members, my neighbors, classmates or fellow parishioners would fit the bill. They did not. I had an insatiable longing to belong to something outside of myself; something bigger that was outside the realm of the life I was leading. The Beatles became the living embodiment of that outward realm and for someone looking for a way out of the mundane life I was living, the fan club dangled that possibility. Despite obstacles I found at every turn, I vowed to continue running the club, no matter what. That stubborn insistence would set the stage for a repeated behavior pattern that permeated the volunteer efforts I made in the subsequent organizations I joined or founded as an adult. It amazes me how patterns like this persist until you recognize them and make a conscious effort to change.

Remember blue carbon paper? Rather than individually typing each newsletter, I used the carbon paper to "mass produce" the February-March newsletter. It looked terrible. I had to find another way to get these newsletters done in a reasonable amount of time. I set my sights on purchasing a mimeograph machine, but to afford it, I had to increase dues. Up they went from ten-cents a month to a whopping twenty-five-cents a month, citing the fact that a dime didn't even cover the cost of stamps. The increase caused a furor, and I lost quite a few members over it, but the club still had a respectable sixty-five members.

Publishing a newsletter wasn't my only challenge. In my desire to bring my Beatles "family" together, I thought it would be fun to host a meeting for the Chicago members. My first attempt was a dismal failure. When only a handful of members showed up, I decided it wasn't worth the effort. It seemed to me that trying to formulate friendships by bringing people of like-mind together would not be as easy as I thought, but even so, my desire to keep trying continued for years.

Our April newsletter was run off on the aforesaid new mimeograph machine, but being inexperienced at running the machine, the quality was inconsistent, with the ink lighter in some areas and darker in others. I hoped the members would persevere and read it. We had some issues that needed to be addressed, such as the ongoing complaints that I was publishing old Beatle news. I explained that I did not have connections to get fresh, hot off the wire news about the Fab Four. It was my hope that what I was sharing may be new to some members, but in my mind the complaint only served to solidify my amateur status.

That same month, our membership grew to a respectable ninety-five members, but only sixty paid their dues. I took it personally when I discovered our members were jumping to other clubs, responding that we did more for our members than other clubs, i.e. "What other club has their officers write personally to you? We take each member as a personal friend, and we hope that you feel the same way." But there was still the issue of lack of support, both monetarily and through article submissions. I lamented we were on the way to the "poor house" and tried to rally everyone to "SHOW US YOU CARE."

By May, the nastiness that was brewing among members started to manifest as hate mail directed at me. It seemed as though every time I turned around, something disappointing happened. Since the meeting I had planned didn't generate much interest, I decided to try a different tactic and make it a destination meeting. I organized a membership trip to WLS Radio studios in downtown Chicago, but again, that trip bombed and once again, I threatened to disband the club unless there was more interest. I didn't realize it then, but this lack of enthusiasm and participation meant no one cared if I disbanded the club or not. No one, but me, that is.

August 1965 provided a double dose of what I've come to call Beatles "infanity." The first was something coveted by every Beatle fan—a ticket to a Beatles concert. I finally saw them in person at Comiskey Park—another Bridgeport landmark—on August 20. They were giving two concerts that day—one in the afternoon and another that night. I had tickets for the evening concert. I didn't exactly have the best seats—we were up in the grandstand—but I was elated that I was one of the 37,000 fans in attendance that night.

Excitement filled the air that day, and I nervously paced the sidewalk in front of my house during the afternoon concert, wondering what the fans were experiencing. I

Ticket Stub to the August 20, 1965 concert at Comiskey Park

tried to take in the fact that the Fab Four were about a mile from where I was standing. Despite the distance, the screaming of the fans at that afternoon concert could be heard all the way to my house and that only intensified my anxiety for what was to come that night.

I never experienced anything quite as thrilling as that concert—with the possible exception of seeing President Kennedy's motorcade when he visited Chicago. When the Beatles first came on to the field to get to the stage, time stood still. Everyone around me was screaming, and I had to stand to see the field. There they were, as real as life, waving and smiling at the fans. I squinted my eyes and rubbed them a few times; in disbelief that this was really the Beatles I was seeing. Those four incredible guys that I had devoted the last year and a half of my life to were real people. It wasn't a fantasy. I didn't make it all up. They were real and I was there, electrified by the excitement of the crowd.

I remember crying more than screaming at that concert, but those weren't tears of joy. They were tears that came from the painful realization of my status. All the hard work that I had done to make the club a success did not earn me any privileges at this concert. I was no better than anyone else sitting around me—fan club president or not. I did not have box seats. I did not get an invitation to the press conference. I certainly did not get an autographed photo. All of those things could have come to me without meeting them, which would have been fine by me. I still firmly believed it was better to remain invisible than run the risk of being rejected. But these feelings exposed a dichotomy. In order to get those box seats, attend a press conference or get an autograph meant I would need to be recognized, yet I was still shying away from any opportunity to meet them in person. Go figure.

I could not deny it. Being relegated to the grandstand pushed every unworthy button I had, and the experience shook me on a deep level that I wasn't aware of until much later in life when I discovered the karmic issues I was working on in this life were acceptance and approval!

Despite those unworthy feelings, my enthusiasm for the group remained high, bolstered by an unexpected gift I received from an unlikely source.

One afternoon shortly after the concert, my father took me to see his photographer friend, Jimmy Ogata. They had been in the Army/Air Force together and continued their friendship after the war. Dad had nearly become partners with Jimmy in his photography business, but he needed $2,000 to buy into the business. Unfortunately, his parents refused to loan him the money. It was one of many lost opportunities my father endured in his life.

Dad nonetheless pursued his interest in photography and built a darkroom off the bathroom in our house. He got all of his supplies from Jimmy, and as a side job, dad photographed weddings and family portraits. I was fascinated by the magic that happened in his cramped, makeshift darkroom and would often ask to come in and watch him develop prints. He eventually taught me how to make copy negatives and develop prints on my own. This enabled me to sell Beatle photos through my club.

One afternoon, I went with dad to Triangle Camera, Jimmy's store/studio on the north side of Chicago. It was a fortuitous trip, for unbeknown to either of us, Jimmy had been one of the photographers at the group's press conference held before their Comiskey Park concert. When my dad told Jimmy that I was a Beatles fan, Jimmy went in the back and brought out three original 8 x 10 black and white photographs he took at that press conference: a close-up of

Paul winking; a shot of John and Ringo behind the microphones with Ringo smiling directly at Jimmy; and a photo
of all four sitting behind the microphones with George
looking soulfully at the camera.

No other fan had those pictures, and to this day I am
honored to have them in my possession. I later thought
how synchronistic it was that I had those photographs. I
wondered, how did it come to be that my father, of all
people, would be friends with a photographer who took
those photos, and who was in the very presence of the four
men I so admired and had dedicated my life to? If my father

had been able to buy into the business with Jimmy, would he have been the one to go to the press conference to take those pictures? It was one of those "so near and yet so far" events that would happen over and over in the coming years. It was one piece of a giant puzzle that wouldn't reveal itself until long after the Beatles were no more.

I no sooner caught my breath from the electrifying experience of seeing them in person, when the Beatles second movie, *Help*, was released a few days later. Like any dutiful fan, I immersed myself in the film multiple times. Watching the Beatles on the big screen in living color was a feast for the eyes. I really didn't resonate with the theme of the movie—I mean, I "got it" and knew the basic plot involved an evil cult and two mad scientists doing whatever they could to steal a giant ring from Ringo's finger, all while the group was attempting to record an album. The ring was an essential element in some sort of religious sacrifice. Ringo was unable to get the ring off his finger, and he, John, Paul and George found themselves being chased all over the globe. As a result, movie goers were able to bask in the breathtaking scenery of the Austrian Alps and the Bahamas, while getting lost in that remarkable soundtrack. Later we learned that the foursome was stoned during the filming. I mean, what did we know? We certainly couldn't tell they were in a "haze of marijuana," nor could we tell they did not especially enjoy making the film.

Even more so, we did not pick up on the deeper meaning of the film. Of that, Tobias Churton writes:

For those who care (and that would not have been the intended audience of Beatle fans) the film is trying to make a link between Christian ideas of sacrifice—the crucifixion atonement doctrine by implication, and the dead killed in the war who sacrificed their lives for the greater good—and that of the palpably balmy sectarians from the "mystic East." This is an interesting idea, but in the context of the madcap setting, it just seems to suggest that the Beatles are more modern, more liberal, and too instinctively intelligent to swallow such ideas, and regard the panoply of ancient religious belief as a daft joke from which they're trying to escape (hence *Help!*). However, one feels that *Help!* is wildly aimed at some vague notion of a false religion, or outmoded superstition and authority, and exploitation of youthful energy by figures of that authority.

All of that aside, it did not impact the day-to-day operations of running the fan club, except to fuel my appetite for all things Beatle-driven. Luckily for me, I met Lori the next month. Lori had been right under my nose the whole time, but because she was a year younger and lived at the other end of the street, our paths did not cross. It was fortuitous that we met in September and discovered our mutual love of the Fab Four. Lori joined the club and that's when things started to change dramatically. Having her at the other end of the block was a definite advantage, but even more so the fact that we were very much kindred spirits and on the same page when it came to writing and managing a club. We were a match made in creative heaven. Her articles were a breath of fresh air, bringing a higher level of writing to the paper than had been there before. I don't think I realized it then, but clearly this was a time in my life when I honed in on my writing and organizational skills, both of which would serve me well as I headed into adulthood.

By September I sent out the Friendship Books I had been promising. This was a book of member's names and addresses that I printed with the intent that members could write to each other, forming friendships. It was my first attempt at networking. I finally got some help with a committee of six girls who were willing to take on some of the work, but their involvement was bittersweet as they were replacing personal friends of mine who were not only leaving the club, but leaving my life.

I remember one very ugly incident when one member of the core group of friends I had went behind my back and organized a meeting in which she convinced the others not only to leave the club, but to cast me out as their friend. When they came to my house to announce they were leaving and I was being ostracized, I burst into tears. I had been emotionally fragile for a long time and this just was the tipping point. I begged them to reconsider and managed to get a few to at least remain friends, but the ringleader looked disgusted that they would even consider remaining my friend. She took a few of the girls I thought were my friends with her out the door and out of my life. I begged for their forgiveness, even though I didn't understand what I had done to make them turn on me. I chastised myself, all out of the desperate hope I could turn things around and keep the club afloat. It was a hard, but important, lesson in conflict resolution and group management. While it was a very painful episode, the lesson did not register enough with me as to avoid making the same mistake with volunteers and friends again.

Getting hit in the soul with this rejection was indicative of the attitude of many fans going from one extreme to the other. We went from unconditional love of the Beatles to commenting about their moral character. But during this period, there were some positive ideas being generated as well. On the subject of our printing news items that were new and of interest to our members, one member entertained the idea that we might find updated Beatle news through an agreement with the national Beatles fan club. "They might be glad to give you info on the Fab Four and also you could be sure of the stories," she wrote. I took that idea to heart and did write to the national club headquartered in New York. I did not receive an immediate response, so I concluded it was a moot point. Little did I know we were in the calm before the storm.

Chapter Three

1966-7: It's All Too Much

1966

The year 1966 seems to have marked something of a watershed in this process of theological deformation. Not only did Time *magazine take notice of the "death of God" school, which certainly impacted on young persons looking for a living deity or deities (and finding something of the kind in the persons of the four Beatles, and subsequently, in their footsteps to India).*

—Tobias Churton, *The Spiritual Meaning of the Sixties*

There was a lot going on between 1965-6 that Beatle fans were unaware of, and yet those events set the tone for what would unfold in the last part of the Beatle years. Churton writes that in 1965-6, George Harrison was driven "into the many arms of Hinduism" because of "the idea that if there is a God, one must see him, one must know him, one must experience him. God must be experientially real in the being of the believer. George found his way to "God-realization" through Vedanta and other philosophical and spiritual traditions in the Hindu wisdom experience."

We didn't know this, of course. But it was Churton's statement about John that explained what we were about to find out: "John's essential spiritual outlook was gnostic, or at least, in 1966, gnostic in the making." Churton goes on to write:

> Around 1966, Lennon concluded that the Jesus whose word was love was one of the enlightened, like the Buddha, who while they had come to "turn on" the world to cosmic consciousness and spiritual awareness, had their words nonetheless twisted by inadequate followers passing the message on like a bucket of water that, by the end of the line hardly had any living water left in it, or, to use another analogy, like a whispered word along a line, that by the end of the line sounds different to the first uttered . . . Such misunderstandings, Lennon believed, characterized the times he was living in, and he felt deeply the need for more, for something else that would make sense of his destiny, a destiny he was aware of but couldn't quite define yet. His own groping for inner freedom found its correlate in everything he heard about the changing world of the Sixties.

In August 1966, the Beatles returned to Chicago for what would be their final concert there. The concert was held once again at the International Amphitheatre, but this time to considerable controversy. John had given an interview to Maureen Cleave, a friend and reporter with the *London Evening Standard*. Her article was published on March 4, 1966 and contained a handful of quotes from their conversation, including John's views on religion.

"Christianity will go," he said. "It will vanish and shrink. I needn't argue about that. I am right and I will be proved right. We're more popular than Jesus now. I don't know which will go first—rock and roll or Christianity. Jesus was all right, but his disciples were thick and ordinary. It's them twisting it that ruins it for me."

By the time John's quote reached the United States, it completely was taken out of context. The headline splashed across the country: John says "Beatles bigger than Jesus." Reaction was swift and outrageous, ranging from Ku Klux Klan protests to burning of Beatles records arranged by Christian radio stations, to death threats.

Because Chicago was the first stop on their 1966 American tour, reporters at the Amphitheatre press conferences on August 11th and 12th pursued the subject with a vengeance. John took the lead in trying to explain what he meant:

> Well, originally I was pointing out that fact in reference to England—that we meant more to kids than Jesus did, or religion, at that time. I wasn't knocking it or putting it down. I was just

saying it as a fact. And it's sort of . . . It is true, 'specially more for England than here. I'm not saying that we're better, or greater, or comparing us with Jesus Christ as a person or God as a thing or whatever it is, you know. I just said what I said and it was wrong, or was taken wrong. And now it's all this.

It did not appear that anyone took into consideration that John had been brought up as a Christian and did believe in God. You would expect someone who was a deep thinker like John to question preconceived notions of God and comment on reaction to religion in the 20th century.

"I believe that what people call God is something in all of us," Ray Comfort quotes John as saying. "I believe that what Jesus and Mohammed and Buddha and all the rest said was right. It's just that the translations have gone wrong."

John was worried about the death threats but despite the reporter's prompting, would not admit he felt as if he were "being crucified." Paul thought the burning of records was "a bit silly" and George called it all a "misunderstanding, which shouldn't be." Ringo just hoped "everyone's straightened out and it's finished."

But the uproar wasn't just in the United States. Comfort writes:

Christians around the world had been dismayed by Lennon's boast in an article in London's

Evening Standard about the popularity of the Beatles, but the singer says he was misunderstood. "It's just an expression meaning the Beatles seem to me to have more influence over youth than Christ," he [John] says.

Despite my penchant for getting on the soap box, I had limited my topics to cooperation within the fan club in terms of submitting articles and paying dues. I did not see myself as one who made controversial statements, and I certainly did not want to become more of a target than I already was. What I didn't understand then was that I wasn't the only one feeling some sort of energetic shift was happening.

After much soul searching, I felt compelled to say something about the Jesus remark, so I addressed it in our September 1966 newsletter. I took the stand that the radio stations that banned the Beatles and wanted to burn their records and books were childish, adding: "They didn't bother to go into complete detail about what John had said," and I defended John's right to his opinion.

Years later I read a quote by George, who as a believer in an afterlife, wondered how those who were behind the record burnings would feel when they died and discovered how wrong they were. That's karma, baby.

I was fortunate enough to be able to see the Beatles this last time at the Amphitheater, one among a privileged group of 13,000 fans in attendance at one of two shows on August 12th.

Ironically, while John was making his controversial comments about the Beatles being more popular than Jesus, a record they released in May of that year had a significant impact on our spiritual growth, although at the time we did not attribute anything remotely spiritual to it. The record was "Rain," released on the flip side of "Paperback Writer," and its meaning went a lot deeper than people complaining about the weather. In *A Hard Day's Write: The Stories Behind Every Beatles Song*, author Steve Turner says of "Rain" that it "was the first Beatles' release that suggested new altered states of consciousness, not just in its lyric but in the music." Turner goes on to say that John was in such a "disoriented state" and "when he heard what sounded like an eastern religious chant coming from his headphones, he knew he had found a sound which accurately reflected his stoned consciousness."

Certainly not all Beatles fans were stoned listening to "Rain," but in so many ways, it, too, reflected our consciousness as well. I remember listening to it over and over, waiting for the end and just closing my eyes and feeling something of some magnitude was happening to me. I just didn't have the words to describe it. Now, when someone asks me what I do, I answer— "I research people in altered states of consciousness." Whoever thought it started with "Rain?"

But that wasn't the biggest musical influence of 1966. "Tomorrow Never Knows" holds that honor. Appearing as the last track on the album *Revolver*, it has stood the test of time and continues to be a source of deep spiritual teachings for me. According to Turner, "Tomorrow Never Knows" was "John's attempt to create in words and sounds a suitable guide track for the LSD experience. The words were borrowed, adapted and embellished from Timothy Leary's 1965 book *The Psychedelic Experience*, which was itself a poetic reinterpretation of the ancient Tibetan *Book of the Dead*."

I remember being intrigued by what was in the *Book of the Dead*. Some of the lyrics from "Tomorrow Never Knows" hit me with a raw truth that penetrated my soul ... "All play the game existence to the end ... of the beginning." If ever there was a seed that would blossom into my passionate pursuit of reincarnation research, that was it.

1967

By 1967, we were battling rumors that the Beatles were breaking up. To lighten the mood, I engaged some of my high school friends to help write articles for the newsletter, but because they weren't die-hard Beatle fans, the newsletter started drifting toward more non-Beatle related columns.

By the middle of 1967, I reluctantly began to run news items about the Beatles taking LSD. I say reluctantly because while it was a legitimate news item, it exposed a side of the group that I knew would cause controversy among our members. Paul had admitted experimenting with LSD in June, creating what Eric Meyers termed "a public relations mess for the band." I didn't feel compelled to comment on it until August. I don't know why I felt "betrayed" with Paul's admission that he took drugs, but later when he said he did not advocate it, I felt better. When I found out later that John and George were also taking drugs, I naively expressed concern for their safety and for the well-being of their future children. I mean honestly—what did I know?

In October, I announced the name of the newsletter would be changed again, this time from *The Beatles Bugle* to *Luv 'n' Stuff*, the name I had used many years earlier in a non-Beatle newsletter I wrote. I even had a tagline: "The newspaper geared towards all Beatle people everywhere." The newsletter had a whole new look with a banner headline, and divided down the middle like the very first issue. The club name was in question, as if I couldn't make up my mind. I was toying with the idea of calling it *The Beatles Love Society*, but the following month I changed it to *The Beatles Love Association*, even though I didn't especially like that name either. This see-sawing of names must have been very confusing to our members, to say the least.

In the fall of 1967, the Beatles were engaged in creating another movie, *Magical Mystery Tour*. It was not especially applauded when it came out, but now is considered an artistic endeavor well ahead of its time. The nearly hour-long production followed a diverse group of people on a British mystery tour. The central characters of the

BEATLES on INDIAN PILGRIMAGE

LUV 'N' STUFF

THE NEWSPAPER GEARED TOWARDS ALL BEATLE PEOPLE EVERYWHERE

| VOLUME 3 | OCTOBER 1967 | NUMB... |

Hi! Hope you like our new look and enjoy the paper. I know that things are hectic now because of school and all, but the Beatles are still supreme, thanks to the many Beatle fans around the country and around the world.

More info on Jason: He was born on August 19 at 3:30 PM, weighing 8 lbs 5 oz and 21 inches long.

If you've received the membership kit and are wondering just WHEN Cyn's birthday is, we're sorry. It's September 10, 1939 which means she recently celebrated her 28th birthday. Other birthdays: Happy 27th to John on October 9, happy 2nd to Zak on September 13 and one to Neil Aspinall on October 13.

If anyone saw the picture of the Beatles in Life sometime ago, that blonde wasn't Maureen. It was Jenny Boyd, Pattie's sister. The article said that it was Maureen, but other reports said that Jenny accompanied them, and although Maureen is a blonde now also, she was in London.

Speaking of that trip to Wales, Cyn was left behind. The report was printed in a British newspaper. I'm quoting from a Cyn Lennon Fan Club Newspaper: "Beatle wife Cynthia just Misses The Mystic Special. The Beatles weekend of peaceful transcendental meditation started off in chaos yesterday. Three of them turned up late for the train at Euston. And JOHN LENNON'S wife, CYNTHIA, got left behind in the scramble. She stood sobbing on the platform as the train pulled out with John yelling thru a window: "Jump! Jump!" But railway police held her back. The Beatles were off to Wales with the Master--Hindu Mystic Mahar-

ishi Yogi - His Holiness to his followers ... The Lennons, George Harrison and wife Pattie and Ringo ran on to crowded platform 13 as the train pulled out and jumped into the last compartment - all except for the tearful Cyn. Neil did drive Cyn to Wales though.

Don't forget to watch "A Hard Day's Night" on October 24. I think it's going to be on NBC. "Help" will be shown either later in the season or next year. Anyone know where I can get a color TV cheap??

The Beatles of course, will be in India by the time you read this. But, they haven't stood still since the untimely death of Brian Epstein on August 27.

They filmed an hour-long color television program intended for world-wide broadcast during the Christmas season. Entitled "Magical Mystery Tour," the show will be the first all-Beatle television production. It promises to be unconventional in theme and treatment. The Beatles have hired a bus and old-fashioned coach-and-four and rambled through southwest England, improvising as they go. The show will be (or is) written, directed and produced by the Beatles themselves. Besides the title song, it will contain four other new compositions. What's the show like? An example is, the quartet will walk into the door of an ancient inn but emerge in a psychedelic studio set.

After their two month visit in India, the Beatles will return to London and set up a school for those who want to "dig the whole bit."

Happy memories...Joanne

film were Ringo and his Aunt Jessie, who has daydreams of falling in love with fellow passenger Buster Bloodvessel. The sequence of scenes was rather disjointed. One scene was a marathon where passengers use different modes of transportation. In another, the tour group walks through a British Army recruitment office with Victor Spinetti, an actor we all recognized from *A Hard Day's Night* and *Help!*, playing an army drill sergeant. Another scene had the tour group crawling into a tiny tent in a field that turns into a projection theatre. My favorite was a restaurant scene in which John plays a waiter who continually shovels what looks like spaghetti onto Aunt Jessie's plate. One of the most memorable scenes, however, was the one in which all four Beatles are descending a staircase in white tuxedos singing, "Your Mother Should Know."

This film was another in a long line of subliminal influences generated by the Beatles. Churton sums it up nicely in talking about the love that is expressed by Aunt Jessie and Buster Bloodvessel:

> What is so moving is not only the love between these two characters but the fact that the Beatles reached out to all people of all ages, whatever they looked like. They were looking beneath the surface and seeing the lonely and gifted souls of people whose characters can make them lonely, and they were seen as whole people, worthy of love and good things. This was an attitude almost unknown in the world of showbusiness, where "love" was almost always the province of either young, healthy, good-looking, possibly white, photogenic boys and girls, or of smart married adults with loving families. The Beatles showed an inclusive love, and like Jesus's parable about

going into the hedgerows to find guests for the real messianic banquet, the Beatles favored the outsiders, the people normally overlooked or frowned on. This was a spiritually Christian gesture in the real sense and shines on today, and will tomorrow.

The other spiritual seed planted in 1967 came in the guise of the Beatles eighth studio album, *Sgt. Pepper's Lonely Hearts Club Band.* I played it incessantly, amazed at how extraordinary each tune was—that is, except for "Within You and Without You." This was my least favorite track, and one I would skip over whenever it popped up. I could not relate to the influence that Indian music had over George. The very sound of it made me shudder on some unseen deep level—so much so, that for years I never "heard" the lyrics. I realize now that whatever bias I had was karmic in nature, because once I got beyond the auditory aspect of the song and into the lyrics, I found it strangely comforting. Years later, I could see how it fit into my burgeoning spirituality.

Ironically, the song encapsulated the very truths I was embracing. That idea, that we are all one, is the foundation upon which most esoteric beliefs exist. Steve Turner writes:

Written as a recollected conversation, the song put forward the view that Western individualism—the idea that we each have our own ego—is based on an illusion that encourages separation and division. In order for us to draw closer and get rid of the 'space between us all', we need to give up this illusion of ego and realize that we are essentially 'all one'.

Another spiritual seed planted in 1967 is one that is an example of subliminal messaging that didn't take hold until twenty years later. It was something George said to a *Look* magazine reporter: "It's up to us to get off that cycle, because it's going to be going around forever. You have to say, 'I've had enough of this roundabout, and I'd like to get on now to something else.' People are making it to the astral plane, but those who don't just keep dying and coming back and dying and coming back. It's all action and reaction."

George went on to say: "The more aware I've become, the more I realize that all we are doing is acting out an incarnation . . . not for yourself particularly but for everyone else, for whoever wants it."

Chapter Four

1968-70: All I Gotta Do

1968

Life magazine may have dubbed 1968 "The Year of the Guru," and *Look* magazine may have called the Beatles the "great scribes of our era," but my head was sorting through more practical matters. I was eighteen and getting ready to graduate from high school. I had had the club for half of eighth grade and all through high school. It was time for some introspection. In June, I wrote a column called *Beatlemania—Today, To Me*. The column was a departure from my usual complaints about dues and newsletter articles. Now I was questioning aloud the wisdom of having gone down the Beatles path in the first place. I wrote:

> It's funny how you look back on days gone by and wonder whatever made you do what you did. Four years ago I was sure I'd still like the Beatles when I was a senior in high school. Today I find myself a 'graduate' and wonder whether I would have been better off to ignore those four

Liverpool lads. In these the formative years, or the years past, I tend to think of the Beatles setting the pace for my personality and my way of life.

I think that the Beatles have set deep within my mind the goals of success. Moreover, they've shown me that there's more to life than what appears on the surface, and most recently, they've shown me how to deal with the generation gap—you merely ignore it; this sense of being your own person, not to strive to please others too much, but to do what is best for your peace of soul . . . It's strange, but to me, not loving the Beatles would have created a far different human being than I am, even though chances are my confusion would have been less. But they were more than a few records playing on my stereo, much more than an electrifying concert, a lot more than pictures on the wall or a TV cartoon series. They have done what others try to do—to touch your inner self and give you a deeper insight into yourself and into the world around you.

So when I'm plagued with the ever-resounding words of 'When will you give this up?' I tend to think—when will I give up breathing or being me? And when I think of all I have by just knowing others like me, life doesn't seem so bad. Even in the pessimistic and sadistic world we live

in, peace and love can shine forth if you believe
it can; if God willing, you can get away from the
spider's web and be with the right people. But
then you know that, don't you? Because you're a
Beatle fan too . . .

Ironically—or should I say symbolically since nothing happens in a vacuum—two weeks before my birthday
the Beatles released "Lady Madonna." I liked that song so
much that I used it for an assignment in which I had to
choreograph an exercise routine for a required gym class
at the University of Illinois. It was way too fast for what I
was asking my group to do, and I regretted that I had not
factored how we could pull off all of the required exercises
to Paul's boogie-woogie piano playing.

But wait, there was a far greater gem here on the B
side of "Lady Madonna." It was George Harrison's "The
Inner Light," for which this book is named. The seeds for
"The Inner Light" were planted by Juan Mascaró, a Sanskrit scholar and Cambridge professor. According to Steve
Turner, Mascaró sent George a copy of *Lamps of Fire,* "a
collection of spiritual wisdom from various traditions that
he had edited. He suggested that George might consider
putting verses from the Tao Te Ching to music, in particular a poem titled 'The Inner Light.'"

The impact this song would have on my life was incal-
culable at the time it was released. I still was not resonating
to the sound of the piece, but I already considered myself a

writer and so it was the words I zeroed in on. I spent hours analyzing them, wondering, for instance, what it meant to say: "Without going out of my door, I can know all things on Earth." I knew what meditation was, but I had not tried it myself.

Meyers calls this bridging—something I was determined to do once my metaphysical career started. How could I take a topic that was taboo by many religious groups and western seekers, and mainstream it enough so it would not be as threatening as they deemed it was to them. This song especially focused in on my desire to connect the physical to the spiritual, to express a more universal view of what life was about. "The Inner Light" discusses the role of the soul and intuitive knowing in a way most had not heard before. George Harrison was truly the "soul" of the Beatles and created the bridge connecting Eastern spirituality with Western beliefs.

Years later when I began my esoteric career, that one sentence— "Without going out of my door, I can know all things on Earth"—would define my work, especially in regression therapy. Doing past-life regression work via Zoom, my clients don't have to leave their homes to have a round-trip ticket to any place and any time period on Earth—or in rare cases, elsewhere. Information that is not available to them in a conscious state, is readily attainable during a regression brought about by hypnosis or guided imagery. I see the tie-in so clearly now, but had no clue when it was presented to me as a teen. Of the power of meditation, Candy Leonard writes:

> It's likely that the Beatles' interest in meditation was a catalyst in the widespread acceptance of the practice. But more pertinent to the fan experience at the time, regardless of whether they were intrigued, "turned off," or neutral about the Maharishi, was that the Beatles had once again given fans something new to think about, talk about, and have an opinion about. A male fan, age seventeen at the time, said the Beatles "made everyone think about aspiring to spiritual enlightenment."

There has been much written about the Beatles' time in India and for the purpose of this book, I am not going to delve into that at any length. I did not resonate to their Indian sojourn when it happened. I may have been intrigued with sacred Hindu texts, but was not drawn to any part of the culture. However, there were elements of that trip that exceeded my resistance toward the Maharishi and the Beatles experience at the Rishikesh Ashram. When talking about the seed of spirituality that was sown for the children of the sixties, George had no doubt that India was its origin.

Author Geoffrey Giuliano captures what I was experiencing: "Harrison's well-publicized spiritual trek to India became a catalyst for a lot of people's own inward journey. Once again, the Beatles led the way."

George may have taken exception to that comment. Giuliano quotes George as saying: "The farther into spiritual life I go, the easier it is to see that the Beatles aren't really controlling any of it, but that something else has now taken us firmly in hand."

George talked about reincarnation in 1968, as evidenced by this quote shared by Ray Comfort: "You go on being reincarnated until you reach the actual Truth … The actual world is an illusion." He also said, "The living thing that goes on, always has been, always will be. I am not really George, but I happen to be in this body."

Tillery explored the path that George and John were on, writing that George and John, "at the pinnacle of their hard-won worldly success, had come to question and devalue its fruits. In their disillusionment they began reading spiritually oriented books such as the Bhagavad Gita, the Bible, and *The Tibetan Book of the Dead*."[1]

Despite the profound teachings that the Beatles were embracing as a result of their affiliation with Indian culture and philosophy, I doubt that the majority of fans "got it" back then. We weren't interested in the Maharishi Mahesh Yogi or anything he was saying. While we may not have said it out loud, we couldn't help but wonder what in the world the Beatles had gotten themselves into and would the day come when they'd abandon this foolishness. And yet George later said something that not only answered that question, but explained it from a reincarnation viewpoint. "I felt at home with Krishna," he said. "I think that's something that has been there from a previous birth."

Tillery goes on to write that "George had an affinity for Indian chanting from the first moment he heard it. He sensed the opening of some subconscious door—as though it brought back memories of a previous life."[2]

I remember when I learned that some of the Beatles abruptly left Rishikesh. Rumors swirled about their sudden departure. At the time I had no idea it had anything to do with them believing that the Maharishi was hitting on the young women at the compound. Imagine my surprise to learn that "Sexy Sadie" wasn't written about a man being made a fool of by a woman, but instead was about the Maharishi himself. Like I said, most Beatle fans tended to live in a bubble and being the president of one of their fan clubs did not give me the inside track on what was really going on.

On the surface it appeared they were ending this phase of their lives, and perhaps for the majority of the group that was true. In reality, for George, this was only the first entrée in a multi-course banquet ahead of him.

In the summer of 1968, Yoko Ono arrived on the scene and Beatlemania, as we knew it, would never be the same. The shock that reverberated among Beatle fans was staggering. I tried to fairly report John and Cynthia's separation, but it was hard not to be biased because the majority of fans were solidly behind John's wife. Kathy Burns, who had been running one of the best clubs out there—a club for Cynthia—announced she was giving it up, "out of respect to Cynthia." We wondered what Cynthia did to have John treat her so deplorably? I speculated that: "Something's happened to John—something no fan can attempt to explain." Indeed, I closed what we considered sad news by stating: "Whoever knew that something so beautiful for Cyn and Julian could end so very, very ugly." Was it so beautiful, or just an expression of our naivete— that childish dream of a happily ever after?

I put out a special edition as to what our members thought of John and Cyn's divorce because I was being bombarded with unsolicited comments. One member said it was a "sad time for all of us" and that it was "a tragedy that won't easily be forgotten." Others begged me not to disband the club over this: "it's too groovy to break up," wrote one member. Others wondered why everyone was blaming John. Some condemned my article, saying my newsletter was a disgrace, while others said they thought John was sick. Some members quit the club over it because they had had it with the Beatles and their perceived lack of morality.

I wonder if those who thought John was "sick" continued to hold that opinion when, in that same year, "Across the Universe" was released. I first heard it on the benefit album for the World Wildlife Fund. I loved it then and love it now. I think of all the Beatles music, this piece greatly added to the foundation of my later beliefs.

One of the elements in "Across the Universe" that I found fascinating, was the repetition of the phrase: "Jai Guru Deva Om." For years, I had no idea what John was singing, and I don't know that other fans did either. It wasn't as if we had the Internet and could ask Google for a song's lyrics. Years later I learned it was a mantra invented by none other than the Maharishi Mahesh Yogi, which roughly translated to "hail to the heavenly Teacher." A mantra is meant to aid in meditation. I would be reintroduced to the power of the mantra in my esoteric training. It seems the time spent with "Sexy Sadie" had a lasting impact on John Lennon, and on me.

While 1968 was a pivotal year in setting the stage for what would blossom many years later, we were still teenagers dealing with life issues that we did not yet have the tools to process. That is why in 1968, when we announced that Paul and Jane Asher had broken their engagement, I was bracing myself for more negative fan reaction. Like Cynthia, Jane had long been considered a favorite Beatle gal by fans. So much was changing. What was next?

It turns out that a lot more was in store for us that year. We received word that The National Beatles Fan Club in New York (Beatles U.S.A. Ltd.) was trying to incorporate all of the independent fan clubs like mine under their umbrella. This was an effort to gain members for the national club, control the news that was being reported, and stop the sale of photographs. We were issued a warning that if our clubs did not become chapters of the national club and pay dues to that organization, we would be sued.

Believing we were being unjustly strong-armed by the national club, I wrote to WCFL DJ Jim Stagg for help. At that time, he wrote a column called "The Stagg Line" in the Sunday edition of *The Chicago Sun-Times*. On September 8th, Jim included the letter I sent him explaining our plight in his column.

> Joanne Maggio of South Lowe Ave., president of a Beatle fan club which boasts 120 members in 15 different states and Canada, is running into interference from the New York headquarters of an organization which is gobbling up all "independent" Beatles fan clubs.
>
> Pressure is being put on Joanne to insist that the members of her club join the New York outfit, with $2.50 dues from all members, "or else."
>
> Joanne wrote to us: "Receiving that letter was probably the biggest blow to the five-year life of the club that I ever experienced. I can well understand if they'd want to get after clubs who are working for profit only, but I can't understand why they're determined to wipe out all the independent clubs. Beatle fans thrive on independent clubs. We have little else, as concerts are forever in the past, records are fantastic but come out less frequently than we'd like,

magazines with them in it are now considered relics and any news of them has to be spread from one fan to another. The Beatles are not the easiest group to love since they meet with so much opposition from those who aren't ready to accept them as yet, but still, there are many of us who haven't changed from that first day in 1964 and who will undoubtedly stick with them no matter what happens.

"I've had this club for nearly five years now. We have 120 members from 15 different states and from Canada. We give them a monthly, 7-page newsletter and sometimes add a bonus of a photo or two. Dues are $1 plus six stamps every six months. Most of the members pay 25-cents a month. Many times, they owe us four, five, six months' dues, then they suddenly drop out. So we never have more than $10 in the treasury at one time. This doesn't worry me as I'm not doing this for the sake of earning money. I'm doing it because I really love the Beatles. I've always wanted to do more for them than merely buy their records or see them at concerts. I know they'll never know who I am, or what I'm doing, and in a way, I don't really want them to.

"Of course, that would be the thrill of a life-time—to have them know I exist—but running this club, meeting all the great Beatle people, well, that's enough for me. The Beatles have made me into the person I am. They've helped me outline my goals and decide what I want out of life. I've tried to make my club into a family affair for all members involved. There have been countless days when I wanted to forget it all, when the opposition was too great, but then I think of all the Beatles have done for me and I want to keep going and try to do something for them. That is why I'm writing, Jim, because if they take away my club and all the independent clubs across the country, we'll be lost. Thank you for reading this, Jim."

He responded in his column:

"We placed several phone calls to New York, Joanne, in an effort to contact the people who are threatening to "sue" you if you don't join up and fork over additional dues. We'll keep you advised of our progress; meantime, we salute you and your members for all your hard work, loyalty and devotion to the Beatles."

A few weeks later I went to see Jim and we talked for quite some time. He said he was behind us all the way and assured us that the national club could not sue us and that we could still sell photos as long as they weren't

"The Stagg Line" column in the Chicago Sun Times

copyrighted. Jim encouraged us to write to the national club and say, "Please sue us" and then inform him of how they responded!

I chose not to stir the pot and for a while, things began to calm down. However, I no sooner thought they had forgotten about us, when a few protest letters sent to them by well-meaning members awakened the sleeping giant and they reappeared, threatening us again. They attempted to convince me that joining them was for the good of my club and that's the way the Beatles wanted it. I ignored their overtures, finding it hard to believe the Beatles gave a damn about what we did. Little did I know that in a short time I'd learn just how wrong I was.

After five years I was growing increasingly tired of all the problems I had with the club. It wasn't the fun experience I thought it would be. Up until then I thought all the aggravation was worth it because the Beatles were worth it. I still felt that way, but now I was wondering what good was a fight if I had no soldiers?

I put in one more word for the independent clubs around the country and asked for everyone's support, but I knew it was a hopeless situation. We were David and the national club was Goliath, and I doubted my slingshot would even make a dent in their armor.

At the time the take-over battle began, there were well over one hundred independent Beatle fan clubs in the United States. My hope was that if all of us stuck together to fight the national club takeover, we had a fair chance of winning. To my dismay, however, one by one the independent clubs folded under the pressure. By November, we were one of only three holdouts.

The national club director, Sandi Morse, sent me a letter trying to convince me of the hopelessness of remaining independent. She enclosed a letter, supposedly from one of the Beatles, suggesting I become a chapter so that there will be only one "club" in the USA. I still couldn't believe any of the Beatles would get involved in something as petty as this, especially John Lennon, who later went on to compose a song declaring "Power to the People." I may have been wrong, but as far as I was concerned, John was focused on much loftier goals than dictating policy to harmless fan clubs.

Sadly, I knew someone from within my club was supplying the New York office with information that was appearing in my newsletter. No one in the New York office was on my mailing list, and yet Sandi knew everything I was publishing. Add to this that the gossip mill was in full swing spreading falsehoods, it became more than I wanted to deal with. With little desire left to fight, I gave in and asked Sandi to send me chapter application information, saying that I would share that with the members and get a vote on it before agreeing to anything. The future of my fan club was definitely on shaky ground.

For Beatle fans it was a dismal time. The December newsletter had news of Yoko's miscarriage, John and Cynthia's divorce becoming final, news that Yoko's estranged husband Tony Cox would be divorcing her, posters of John and Yoko in the nude, and the emergence of Linda Eastman as Paul's new love interest. With so many changes happening, and my inability to report news from reliable sources, I felt I had no choice but to become a chapter of the national organization. I tried to look on the bright side. If there was a plus side to becoming a chapter, it was that the national club had material that I could only dream of giving to my members—all top-notch things like 8 x 10 b/w glossy photos that no one had seen elsewhere.

Nonetheless, I had to ask everyone to send me $2.50 to cover a year's dues. I needed twenty members to do so before I could be an official chapter, so it was important for me to convince my members to send that money in, plus continue to pay dues to me. It felt like a herculean task. To sweeten the pot, I decided to lower our dues to make it more affordable for members during this turnover period. I wasn't certain I could convince my members to join the national club. So many of them had expressed disillusionment with the Beatles, especially with John and Paul, whose life choices were causing additional friction between fans and their parents.

Other events in 1968 added to the grim realities of our lives. Martin Luther King, Jr. and Robert F. Kennedy were assassinated that year, and we were still dealing with the Vietnam war. It felt as if the entire planet was shaking, making it hard to gain any equilibrium. There was no escaping the enormous changes happening around us.

But then, there was George Harrison, stepping into the spotlight, as if to say— 'It's okay. We're okay. Just follow my lead.' Even John noticed this when he said that George wasn't a mystery, but the mystery inside of George was huge. John said watching George gradually uncover that mystery was interesting to him.

Certainly I did not know it then, but years later, I would come to wonder if that is how I appeared to those around me, witnessing my own emergence into a greater spiritual dimension.

1969

By February of 1969, *The Beatles Love Association* attained the status of becoming an official chapter of Beatles (U.S.A.) Ltd., which early in the year changed its name to The Official Beatles Fan Club [A Division of Apple Music Publishing Company]. There were some pluses to this to be sure, but on the downside, we were prohibited from accepting anyone in our chapter who were not members of the national club. As a result, we lost quite a few members, but I decided it was a necessary price to pay to stay afloat.

My editorials became more philosophic. As February was the fifth anniversary of the Beatles arrival in the U.S., I wrote an article "On Beatle People in 1969" that looked at the very nature of fandom, from a rather dark perspective. I wrote that fans existed in a vacuum of "a lonely depression with slight intervals of uplifting happiness—enough to last them through the lull." Was I talking about fans? Or was I really talking about me?

March 1969 was quite a month in Beatles history because we had two weddings to report: Paul and Linda's and John and Yoko's. I was trying to keep my head above water, with attending a full load of classes at the University of Illinois/Chicago Circle and working part-time as a legal secretary. I was still churning out a monthly seven-page newsletter, trying to keep up with the policies of the national club, answering mail, handling the club's finances, and selling items through the club's newsletter.

In May 1969 I dropped a real bombshell on the members when I asked what they thought of the idea of turning the *Beatles Love Association* into *The Official Paul McCartney Chapter*. Beatles (U.S.A.) Ltd. was allowing one "official" club per Beatle and believe it or not, Paul's was available. I knew that the majority of fans in my club were Paul fans and to enable the chapter to grow, I needed to capitalize on that market. I promised not to ignore the other three Beatles and said the newsletter would remain the same with the exception that our name would be different. I did not want to face a mass exodus over this decision, but in my gut, I knew it was the right move to make.

Despite a loud protest, *The Official Paul McCartney Chapter* debuted in June 1969. I tried to be as diplomatic about my decision as possible and wrote the following under "Club News" in an effort to address member concerns:

> Before we were an obscure Beatle fan club, one among many, and our membership never got over the 100 mark, while specialized clubs such as George's official club, boasted well over 900.

LUV STUF

The Official Paul McCartney Chapter c/o Joanne Maggio, President
2838 South Lowe, Chicago 60 ...

JUNE, 1969   BEATLE NEWS

By now you've probably already heard the new single from the boys (john & Paul to be exact) entitled "The Ballad of John and Yoko." The single has already sold nearly 200,000 copies in Chicago, yet has been banned on a Chicago station, WLS because of the phrase in the single, "Christ, you know it ain't easy." Luckily, WCFL and 32 other stations around the country are playing it. The flip side, "Old Brown Shoe" is one of George's efforts and if you aren't partial to BALLAD, the purchase of the record is worth it in view of OLD BROWN SHOE.

When the new Beatle album comes out in the fall (or late summer) we'll also be getting some sort of book, contents and author still a secret.

As you must know, John & Yoko went off to the Bahamas to have a bed-in, but the heat was too much for them and they went off to Toronto. John says he would have preferred to come to the U. S. for the bed-in, but since his visa was taken away, he chose Toronto instead. There, he and Yoko stayed in a $300.00 a day suite and received visitors from their beds. Among the visitors were Tom Smothers, (who said something like "Ono is a no-no," Petula Clark and Timothy Leary. Both Governor Rockefeller and Senator Edward Kennedy politely declined the invitation to go there, and Canada's Prime Minister said that he thought people could spend their holidays more profitably by climbing mountains.

Speaking of the visa problem (and I'll try and get in an article about that in the next newsletter) remember that John and George can get them back if they simply reapply for one. They can write to the Attorney General (and don't YOU go doing it) and apply for a waiver. In George's case it will be easy, as he's been off the stuff for years. Or, they can petition the American consul there in London. John had another application in but he withdrew it for some reason. So please stop condemning the U. S. government!

George is now in London working, and Rich is in the Bahamas for a vacation, having just finished making "Magic Christian" in both London and a few scenes in New York.

In an interview with KYA (California) DJ Tom Campbell, John mentioned that he would be putting out a record called, "Give Peace a Chance" which he'll record as soon as he can.

Paul's supposedly somewhere in Europe now touring.

By the way, speaking of touring, John seems determined to tour again, once he gets his visa back, and wants to play all the big cities. George & Rich are still against it, and Paul hasn't said one way or the other.

Did I mention last time that John will be playing the part of Jesus Christ on BBC for some weeks?? I'm not sure whether he has accepted or not, but some sources confirm that he has.

Some of the new songs on the new album (Beatle album) will be Maxwell Silver Hammer" , "Maggie May", "Teddy Boy" and Heather will be on some of the recordings.

In the rumor-don't-believe-it-til-you-see-it department, Paul has agreed to be photographed in the (forgive the expression) nude and his picture to appear as the design of a single 45 in England; the title of the 45 EP is: Across the Universe.

Allen Klein is now the Beatles' financial adviser and business

June 1969 Newsletter

I'm not asking for a club with over 900 people in it, but for me, for the time that's put into the club, stagnation is defeat, and the only possible way I could see our growth is by making our club into one for Paul . . . I think I've made the right decision and I hope that you will have enough faith and trust in me to feel the same way. I wouldn't steer you wrong and I think you'll enjoy the chapter just a 'little bit better.'

For some reason, my success at running a Beatles fan club continuously for over five years, and perhaps because of my tenacity in holding off the takeover and eliciting the help of DJ Jim Stagg, caught the attention of the powers that be in New York. In July 1969, I made the announcement that I had been appointed by Sandi Morse at Beatles (U.S.A.) Ltd. to be head of all the U.S. Chapters. Maybe they thought that I would be better off working for them than against them—or maybe they just wanted to keep an eye on me. In any case, I was thrilled to add "National Chapter Director" to my resume. I saw this as an avenue of interacting with all the clubs throughout the country. I envisioned swapping newsletters, ideas, and then passing them on for the betterment of all—a sort of co-op among the fan clubs so to speak.

With this position I was given a stipend of $25 a month to pay for postage and supplies. It was never enough, but it did give me bragging rights to say I was on Apple's payroll. How many fans could say the same?

I also had the enviable position of being in charge of "copyrighting" all the photos that were being sold by individual chapters, which meant I had to be sent one copy of every photo. I developed a system to keep track of the

photos to ensure that no two chapters were selling the
same ones. I still have those photos to this day.

As much as I was proud of myself for having made
what I thought to be sound business decisions for my
club, in truth I had no business running *The Official Paul
McCartney Chapter*. I didn't feel at all passionate about what
Paul and Linda were doing together professionally. When
you think of celebrity mania today, spouses are generally
not as derisive a figure as they were when the Beatles were
popular. Being a Beatle wife garnered pop status for Pattie,
Maureen, Linda and Yoko (and before them for Jane and
Cynthia) with fan clubs popping up for them as readily
as they were for their husbands and/or boyfriends. In the
Beatles family atmosphere we created, we saw no separation in our affection for one without the other. Nonetheless, it wasn't a good thing for a club president to express
any kind of bias and if he or she did, it was best to step
aside. After all, you're not really serving the members by
promoting animosity toward the wife of the man you pro-
fess to be so devoted to.

I sensed with the arrival of Linda and Yoko, that the
Beatles we had come to know and love and build our
worlds around was being torn apart. Their energy was
now infused into the foursome, creating more than a little
tension between four men who used to be close friends.
I abhorred the thought that these two women had that
much power and because I did not see that power being
used in a positive way, I could not support either one of

them. Feeling that way, I should have stepped aside then, but I stubbornly held on to not only my chapter, but also my position as National Chapter Director.

Although I promised my members that I would include news on the other three Beatles despite our being Paul's chapter, in August I received a letter from headquarters telling me that the four clubs that were for each of the Beatles could only sell photos and run articles on that particular Beatle. With this edict seriously cutting into our profits, I had to come up with new ideas to generate an income—all of which had to be Paul-related. I came up with the idea of selling Paul stationery, offering 20 sheets of blue 8-1/2 x 11 sheets of paper with Paul's name running down the left side of the paper in Old English lettering, plus 10 sheets of plain paper and 20 envelopes. The quality was horrendous and the whole idea bombed, but that did not mean I gave up on finding ways to keep us afloat financially.

By now, all of the girls who had been with me from the start had long since left the scene and new friends came in to replace them. In late summer, I decided it was time to organize another meeting which was held on August 30 at The Palmer House, one of the most prestigious hotels in Chicago. I had had little luck hosting meetings at my home in previous years, but here I was at age 19 planning a meeting downtown. This was really grown-up stuff!

To my surprise, the meeting was an enormous success, despite the unusual makeup of the group. I had sent out announcements to 700 Illinois members of the national club. One hundred showed up, each bringing a friend, resulting in a room that was overflowing with 200 fans. It was a rather eclectic group. Some came mistakenly believing this was a luncheon meeting. When they learned no food was being served, they left. Others decided to leave because they thought we were going to have a debate on the lives of the Beatles and when it was apparent we were there just to meet new friends and have fun, these controversy-loving fans decided it wasn't for them. Some "hippy-types" came and I was appalled at how they were dressed, considering the meeting was held in one of Chicago's most elegant hotels. We had set up a dress code, only because we wanted to create a favorable impression with the management as mature young adults rather than "crazy Beatle fans." Two girls showed up dressed in denim blue-jean bell-bottoms, saggy jersey tops, stringy hair and bare feet. Their attitude was as bad as their wardrobe, making insulting comments to whatever was being said. They were the antithesis of everything we stood for, and although now I can see how judgmental we were, I did learn a big lesson about opening myself up to a crowd of strangers who were not all operating with the same agenda.

The girls who crashed the meeting continued to cause problems for several months. While I did not shy away from controversy, I wondered how to handle this growing chasm between Beatle fans. I reasoned that if everything were out in the open, we could maturely address the issues that were dividing us.

It became obvious to me that the stress and strain of the Beatles relationship with each other was filtering down to their fans. We were echoing the discord of the group. They weren't getting along, so neither were we. They were drifting apart based on different lifestyle choices and so were we. We may not have seen it at the time, but we were mirroring everything our "lads" were doing. Like a bacterium that eats away at healthy tissue, there was a parasite eating away at Beatlemania.

The infighting among members continued to increase, with letters being sent to me reflecting the frustration and intolerance of fans for each other. Those who loved John, regardless of what he did or said, were criticized by those who did not agree with his views or his actions. Those who liked Yoko were blasted by those who hated her. The same was happening with Paul fans. There was the pro-Linda group and the anti-Linda group. I had unwittingly allowed the newsletter to become a platform for these diverse groups to throw mud at each other. We were once united in our love for the Beatles. Now we were divided into sects, each hating the other, each believing the other was intolerant and narrow-minded. Instead of "peace" and "love" and "flowers," we were hurling hateful expletives at each other. "You say you want a revolution?" We had a full-blown war on our hands and none of us realized it was a no-win scenario. By December I had had enough of the bickering and hate mail and decided to issue a policy statement that our newsletter would not be used for hateful purposes by either side.

Ironically, the spiritual side of our involvement with the Beatles continued. In late November, George's three-record set, *All Things Must Pass*, was released. That music provided comfort on a deeper level than I knew existed within me. I obviously wasn't the only one who felt that way. Writing about the album, Geoffrey Giuliano states: "Not only was the album a gripping musical masterpiece but it was also imbued with an important spiritual message. Inspired by Harrison's homespun philosophy, young people everywhere began looking inside themselves for their own answers."

1970

By 1970, the writing was on the wall. *The Beatles Book Monthly*, a well-respected magazine on the Beatles that was published in England, was being discontinued. I had a subscription to this publication and relied on it for what I thought was accurate news. Ironically, in 2021 as I was watching the Beatles documentary, *Get Back*, I recognized the magazine in the hands of various Beatle members. They were laughing as they were reading articles about each other, a sort of cheeky "did you know you did this . . . or said this?" It was then that I realized that what I had considered one of the more trustworthy magazines about the Beatles contained as many falsehoods as the tabloids do today. It only added to my ongoing question of what was true, what was someone's fabrication of the truth, and how could we tell the difference?

Changes were happening everywhere, including with the demographics of our fan club base. It was growing younger.

Addressing the crowd gathered at one of our downtown meetings

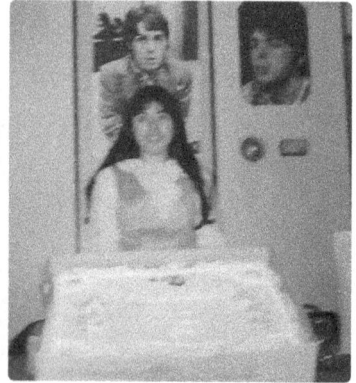

Holding cake commemorating our club anniversary

Our second meeting downtown, this time at the Executive House Hotel, brought out about 125 teenyboppers. I was nearly twenty and found it hard to relate to kids who were barely thirteen years old. Where were my peers? I wondered if I, and my new friend Vikki Paradiso—the area secretary for Illinois and someone who played a pivotal role in the club and in my life at that point—were the oldest living Beatle fans in America? Perhaps it was just that those our age, young adult women, had gone on with their lives, finishing school, starting careers, pursuing life in the real world. I looked around the room at the kids who were rushing the photo table or who sat with blank looks on their faces when we tried to engage them in conversation and I realized the passing years had taken me to a whole new place.

Terri Schultz, who wrote the "Our Town" column for *The Chicago Tribune*, heard about our meeting and sat in the back observing. Her column addressed the issue of the growing age difference between the "old fans" and the new crop of teenyboppers. She interviewed me and wrote the following:

> One hundred twenty-five of the fan club's loveliest girls and a few of the shyest guys turned up for a recent Beatles meeting in the Executive House, where pretty Joanne Maggio, 20, president of the Official United States Paul McCartney chapter, explained the problem:
>
> "Now take Yoko (John Lennon's wife). We in the old faction don't approve of her. We feel the whole thing is degrading. But the 12- and 13-year-olds, and the peace-love faction, they're all for her. They put Paul on a pedestal. They see him as pure and bubbly and innocent. They even call him 'Paulie.' God! He'd die if he heard that. They forget he is a grown man and can make

mistakes, which he has," she sighed. "Six years with the club, and for what? It's such a shame how the Beatles have changed."

Cringe, cringe, cringe. Did I really say that? Did I really make those incredibly judgmental, naïve statements for the entire world—well at least *The Tribune* readers—to see? Maybe it *was* time for me to get out.

But, in the immortal words of Michael Corleone in *The Godfather*: "Just when I thought I was out, they pull me back in!" The following month I was scheduled to go to New York with a few friends. It was my first trip without my parents and my first time on a plane. Growing up in Chicago, I was confident I could maneuver in the Big Apple, although I wasn't prepared for the rudeness of the cab drivers. "Go home" the cabby said matter-of-factly as he took us to the Howard Johnson Hotel just a few blocks from the Beatles national fan club office. Was this going to be the same message I'd get at Beatles' headquarters?

Beatles (U.S.A.) Ltd. headquarters in New York

My appointment to meet with Sandi Morse and Rusty Rahn happened to be on my 20th birthday. Quite a gift, I thought. I arrived at their office at 1700 Broadway feeling like the Midwest country bumpkin in the big city, despite my Chicago roots. I went up to the 40th floor and when the elevator doors opened, I saw a door with the APPLE logo on it. Feeling as if I "belonged," I opened the door and announced myself to the receptionist. Sandi came out to greet me and brought me inside.

I had expected to see row upon row of desks manned with secretaries typing away. Instead I walked into a near-deserted floor of offices. I met Rusty, the Assistant Director, who would soon be sole director, and their three part-time helpers. But that was it. Five people were running a fan club of nearly 40,000 members. I had been prepared to voice the complaints of our members about the national club, but having a hard time managing three hundred members,

Celebrating my 20th birthday in the Beatles' New York office

I could not fathom what it was like to oversee 40,000. Out of sympathy, I respectfully remained silent.

Sandi and Rusty were gracious and gave up most of their day for me, even treating me to lunch at the Americana Hotel. They did a good job of convincing me of the realities of running a club that size on a mere $2.50 per member basis. As employees, they had to report to Allen Klein and from what they said, the rules were stringent and he ran the organization with an iron fist. With so much unbelievable red tape and bureaucracy in place, I was amazed they got anything approved at all. I came there to protest, but left a staunch supporter of their work and renewed my promise to assist in any way possible just to keep things running.

The empty offices should have been my first clue that we were definitely on a downward spiral. News from England should have been my second clue. In my April 1970 issue I reported on a story appearing in *Newsweek* that Paul had quit the Beatles. I followed up with quips from *The Chicago Sun-Times* and other media outlets across the country that picked up on the story. Paul was cited as saying he was leaving because of "personal differences, business differences, musical differences, but most of all, because I have a better time with my family." He supposedly said he did not foresee ever writing another song with John Lennon again. "My only plan is to grow up," he was reported to have said. Was he trying to tell us something?

The news media said the break had been a long-time coming, and put the blame on Allen Klein who had come in to handle the Beatles' financial affairs. Paul not only did not like Klein, but felt he had botched the Beatles' business. But blame was also put at the doorstep of Yoko and Linda, which is something fans had bought into for months. Derek Taylor, press officer of Apple, told *Newsweek*: "It was easier for four boys to get together than four men and four wives." Maureen and Pattie had been around since nearly the beginning, so it was doubtful they were having any negative influence on their husbands, but a spokesman for one of the Beatles made the suggestion that since Paul married Linda, he had been very much influenced by her adding— "You would never find nude frontal pictures of Paul and Linda anywhere." Paul had objected to the influence of Yoko over John and to the sale of lithographs depicting John and Yoko having sex, which Paul felt went against all the Beatles stood for.

Allen Klein said Paul was under contract to Capitol Records until 1976 and he intended to hold him to it, but another spokesman said the only valid contract Paul had was with the Beatles and their only contract was with EMI. If Paul could not work without permission from the other Beatles, then they could not work without permission from him.

To exert his newfound independence, Paul released his first solo album, *McCartney*, which included Linda's harmonies and Paul playing every musical instrument. John formed the Plastic Ono Band with Yoko and focused his attention on their peace campaign. None of us seemed to know what in the world Ringo and George were doing, but we went on with business as usual, hoping this was only a temporary break that would be healed when everyone got their need for a solo-venture out of their system.

As for me, I was once again in defense mode. Many members believed I hated Linda and that my articles were biased against her. I explained repeatedly that I did not hate Linda and that I was merely reporting whatever news I could come by as to the status of the group. We were all holding our breath, waiting for something positive to come out of this and when I went to write the May issue, I started with a portion of a lyric from Paul's "Let It Be:" "... and though they may be parted there is still a chance that they may see ..."

In early May, George's "I Me Mine" was released. Even if you lived under a rock, it was obvious what this song was about. About George's song, Steve Turner writes: "It was his belief that it is our preoccupation with our individual egos—what 'I' want, what belongs to 'me', what's 'mine'—that prevents us from being absorbed into the universal consciousness, where there is no duality and no ego." Those of us listening to it believed its lyrics were reflecting the management troubles the group was facing. That sense of entitlement, of selfishness, of only caring about fulfilling the desires of the ego, is a sentiment that can be applied to life today. It truly captured the darker side of humanity.

The Beatles movie, *Let It Be*, was released in mid-May. The 90-minute color film documented how the group went about recording an album. When I went to see the flick, the audience was made up of primarily young kids, and I knew they didn't have a clue what was transpiring. There were certainly many scenes and conversations where astute Beatles fans could read between the lines and see the strain in the group, but for the younger fans, it wasn't obvious at all.

My May issue held out some hope that they'd remain together. I printed a portion of an interview Paul had given in which he said he was upset that the headlines read: "Paul McCartney Quits the Beatles!" He said he never meant it to take on that connotation and he reiterated what the national club was telling its members—that he merely wanted to go off on his own and do something constructive instead of waiting around. Paul said he was hoping that John would come back and say 'okay lads, I'm back, let's get to work,' but Paul feared he wouldn't do that in the foreseeable future. With his creative juices in full swing, Paul had the urge to do something on his own. Even George, he pointed out, had indicated he wanted to do a solo album. The message was—hold on. Things aren't quite over yet. It was news we had been longing to hear.

While my trip to New York had bolstered my spirits, so did our June 20th meeting, scheduled to coincide close to Paul's June 18th birthday. Sixty fans showed up and we managed to actually get club business done. I made an announcement to the members that I had decided to give up the chapter and appoint a new president. It took a few members aback and the unexpected protest caught me off guard. The members begged me to stay. Many stepped forth and pledged to help, which was quite gratifying. Although I was tired and felt it was time to move on, I was buoyed by the belief that I'd have help so I agreed to continue.

Over the next few months, I continued to deal with the factions within the club, going so far as to writing a three-part editorial on how Paul fans were divided and why. Despite promises at the June meeting, nothing much changed. My parents were beginning to pressure me to give up the club and the criticisms I was getting from friends and family were that I was "too old" to be doing this anymore.

In September 1970 I went back to New York and met again with Rusty and told her of my decision to give up my club. She asked me to stay on as National Chapter Director, which I agreed to do. When I came home, I told the membership that I was looking for a new president for Paul's club and would entertain all offers. None came. Paul's admittance that he had, indeed, left the Beatles, and the continued infighting among members, did not make the presidency of a Paul McCartney Fan Club very palatable to my remaining members.

Yet while the issue of running the club appeared to have an impending end date, the influence of the Beatles did not. On a subliminal level, they continued to plant seeds in our generation. As Churton puts it, ". . . it had certainly been brought home sharply by the end of the decade, that in some quarters the Beatles were being taken *too* seriously." He went on to say that Timothy Leary, "personally, and perhaps foolishly, elevated the Beatles to 'avatar' status in his cheerful psychedelic rhetoric." That was certainly the case with the fans in my circle and definitely the case with me.

Chapter Five

1971: Bangla Desh, Bangla Desh

1971

In August 1971, I produced a special issue I called "Pilgrimage," which chronicled my experiences before, during and after the August 1, 1971 Concert for Bangladesh at Madison Square Garden in New York City.

My attendance at that concert was made possible by my close friend at that time, Linda Woods. Linda was a native New Yorker with an attitude that was a force to be reckoned with. Ironically, she and I connected when she started sending me hate letters that, as I remember, were quite intense. Rather than ignoring her, I continued to engage until somehow, we managed to hash out our differences and become fast friends. Linda was president of her own fan club, *Five Bites of the Apple*. She was a dear and got tickets for me and two fellow Beatle fans traveling with me.

Like Linda, those of us who had chapters had been told by Laura, the new director of the national club, that Allen Klein would be getting a block of tickets for the fan club presidents and area secretaries. It was no secret that Klein disliked the fan club, so this caveat sounded like a long shot. According to Sara Schmidt, author of *Dear Beatle People: The Story of the Beatles North American Fan Club*, when Klein became the Beatles manager in 1971 he found the business in shambles. Schmidt wrote: "John had said, 'Apple needs a new broom,' and Klein was prepared to make a clean sweep. He dismissed staff and ended all lavish hospitality. He did this in London and New York City, firing employees, and eliminating excess spending. National fan club director of Beatles (U.S.A.) Ltd. Sandi Morse kept her job."

Schmidt goes on to reiterate that Klein was not a fan club supporter, and quoted Laura as saying: "Allen disliked the club. He said there was to be no advertising for the club. He eventually put an end to *The Beatles Book Monthly* . . . I was asked to be interviewed on BBC radio about the fan club, but Klein would not allow it. I was able to talk about being a Beatles fan, but not about the club. There was a TV show in New York that wanted to do a show on fan clubs, but Allen [Klein] would not allow me to do it either."

So when Laura asked Klein to let the area secretaries and club presidents buy a block of tickets directly from the fan club office, and mentioned this to us in her correspondence, it wasn't surprising that he wouldn't allow this. None of us were expecting free tickets—just the opportunity to purchase the tickets and sit together as a group. After all the years of service asking nothing in return, we thought this was a reasonable request. Those who volunteered for the club, including myself as National Chapter

Director, only learned that the block of tickets was not available after we arrived in New York City for the concert. Fortunately, Linda must have had a sixth sense about it and decided to get tickets on her own "just in case." Laura and Rusty, as Apple employees, got third-row seats for themselves and their boyfriends at the evening concert.

It was a tough decision for me to go to New York. I was attending classes that summer and the concert was scheduled right before midterms, but the chance to see George perform, meet up with the friends I had made through the fan club, and get away from parental and school pressure for a few days was too good to pass up.

After checking into the Howard Johnson's, my two traveling companions (one being the president of another Chicago-based Beatles Fan Club) went with me to the fan club office, arriving there around 1:30 p.m. Everything had changed. There were new faces including some even Laura didn't know. The dress code had lightened somewhat, but the atmosphere was stifling and unfriendly. I sensed we were a drain on Laura's time and patience. There were moments of awkward silence, each of us wishing to address the elephant in the room and ask her if she got the tickets. When I finally broached the subject, Laura shook her head and said that very afternoon Allen Klein told her that the outside fan club people—chapter presidents and area secretaries—would not get tickets but those working in the office would receive two each. He told her that he could not give us tickets because celebrities had paid up to $500 for tickets (the ticket Linda got for me was all of $5.50) while others, like Senator Edward Kennedy, David Frost, Dick Cavett and Andy Williams couldn't get tickets at all, so how did we expect Apple to give tickets to us?

Laura went on to defend her boss, saying Mr. Klein was paying for the tickets for all Apple employees and was not getting paid anything for the concert, so he could not be expected to do any more. Laura insisted she tried her best. When I reminded her that I was indeed on Apple's payroll and therefore should be entitled to a ticket, she gave me a curt no. I was told that I lived and worked in Chicago and there's a difference in working at your home than there is in working at Apple Corps in New York. Yes, I thought—there is a difference. They come to an office from 9 to 5 and that's it. I go to school, then a part-time job, and then home to work on the fan club. What was it that Sandi Morse once said that Paul supposedly wanted me to know—that I "wouldn't be forgotten in the end?" Not forgotten? More like, not remembered in the first place! But then, I don't believe Paul ever said that. I doubted he even knew who I was.

I decided to change the topic and talk to Laura about club business. I gave her some ideas on how I thought my position as National Chapter Director could be improved. I also mentioned that her predecessor had told me that they would print stationery for me with my name and address on it. Laura looked at me as if I had two heads. She seemed bothered that I had mentioned the stationery, but went through the forms in her inbox as if to placate me. I knew the paperwork for such a request did not exist but I let her pretend she was looking for it.

It seemed to me that lying was second nature at the fan club. In Sara Schmidt's book, *Dear Beatle People,* she discussed one such lie perpetrated on the chapter presidents and area secretaries. Sara reported that Sandi had gone to London for meetings at the Apple offices. Sandi claimed she had met all four Beatles there, but Sara cast some doubt on that, saying it may have been she met them separately, as Paul had not been to the Apple offices for quite some time and the other three would regularly come and go from the offices. Sara wrote: "It was essential to keep the image of The Beatles as friends. To avoid divisive issues Sandi told U.S. fans a white lie. Sandi informed the area secretaries and chapter presidents that she'd brought back many fantastic items for the fans. One of these items was a surprise special Christmas gift. It was a small cardboard Apple records cube. On three sides, there were images of a Granny Smith apple. One side was a full apple, the next had two bites taken out, and the third had the apple's core. The bottom had all four Beatles' autographs. The top of the cube said, "A Merry Christmas and Happy New Year from Apple." Sandi told the area secretaries in a letter included with the gift, "It was indeed a pleasure having them sign all of your Apple Box Christmas Cards."

Sandi pawned them off as real autographs and I believed her. I mean, why wouldn't I? That cube became my most treasured possession. Fast forward many years later, and my

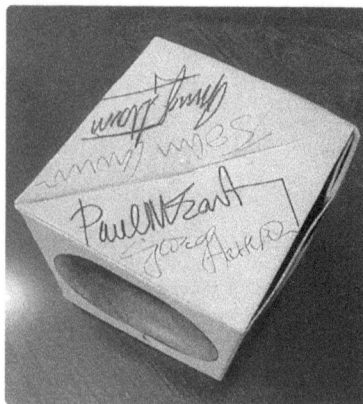

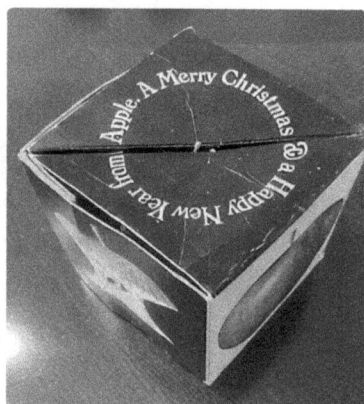

husband, who is an avid sports collector, insisted we get the signatures authenticated. He had gotten tickets to the Antiques Roadshow when they were filming in Richmond, Virginia. I protested, telling him I really didn't want to find out that they were, in fact, forgeries. Let me keep my dream! I eventually gave in and took the cube to the Roadshow. While we stood in line to get it authenticated, I was sure they'd be impressed that I had the actual signatures of the four Beatles. But it didn't take long for my worst fears to be realized. After examining the signatures under a microscope, the authenticator announced that the signatures were fake. I protested, because to my eye, they looked real enough. She seemed sympathetic and tried to convince me they were stamped. I wondered, how could they be "stamped" when some looked like they had been written with a ball point pen and others with a marker. I was absolutely shattered and to this day, haven't forgiven my husband for insisting we have it authenticated!

In reading Sara Schmidt's account of the Apple cube, she, too, acknowledged the signatures were a fake. "When Beatles autograph experts look at the signatures today, they believe that they are not the genuine autographs of John, Paul, George or Ringo. Nonetheless, with so few of these cubes given out (55), the area secretary Apple Christmas Cube is still a highly collective piece of Beatles memorabilia."

Of course, I didn't know any of this at the time I was in Laura's office, but listening to the things she was saying and watching her disingenuously go through the motions, I became so disillusioned that I claimed hunger for my excuse for ending our meeting.

The more I thought about it, the more ridiculous it seemed that Laura actually believed Allen Klein didn't give tickets to Senator Kennedy and the other host of celebrities she rattled off in order to make sure she and her co-workers could go to the concert. Were they trying to make fools of us? I felt very small indeed, but that was nothing compared to how I would feel the next day.

On Saturday we walked back to headquarters. From there we went to the Park Lane Hotel where George, Ringo and the other performers were staying. There were a few fans standing in front of the hotel, including Linda Woods, whom I met face-to-face for the first time.

Linda was an old pro at standing for hours in front of a building where one of the Beatles was staying, living, recording, or performing, but as I alluded to earlier, it was a humiliating experience for me. It was ridiculous to be standing idly in front of a hotel waiting for a "celebrity" to appear. It felt as though I had a big scarlet letter on my chest—this one a big "F" for FAN.

Yet somehow, the more we talked to the kids standing there, the less humiliating the experience became and within an hour or two we had become a part of the group, sharing stories. To amuse ourselves, we would stare back at the passersby and answer their inquiries of "Who's here?" with "Mickey Mouse." We even verbally pounced on someone we perceived to be a Park Avenue debutante who told her beau: "Oh I waited for them six years ago" with our reply: "We're *still* waiting, lady!"

I stood in front of that hotel from 10:00 that morning until 7:30 that night to see one-half of the group I had devoted nearly eight years and, by my estimation, nearly $10,000 to. During all that time we were not allowed to sit down. The guards at the Park Lane pushed and shoved us, people persistently mocked us, and under my breath, I kept muttering: "I'm National Chapter Director." We talked to Tom, John Lennon's chauffeur and we talked

Mal Evans, the Beatles' Road Manager

to Mal Evans, the Beatles road manager, but no one would tell us when George and Ringo were coming out.

The humidity reached 91-percent and it rained twice. Some kids who had driven in from Chicago were lying on their car across the street. A guy named Sam said he'd rather see Elvis Presley. I remembered Sam because despite his nonchalant attitude about seeing one of the Beatles in person, he nearly knocked me over to get to George when he finally emerged from the hotel.

A group of fans arrived who had time-warped straight out of 1964. They asked juvenile questions, jumped up and down when a mere name was mentioned and then, when George and Ringo finally came out, they produced the usual screaming and pounding on the limo door. And there I was, standing there, muttering "I'm National Chapter Director" and hoping the pizza I had eaten earlier wouldn't come up on me.

Maureen and Pattie came out of the hotel around four o'clock, supposedly to go shopping. They waited by the hotel door until the limo pulled up, hurried in and sped away before we could see or talk to them—if that was even a possibility.

As the crowd grew bigger, I felt smaller and very much apart from everything. Why I stayed, I don't know. Maybe for the same reason some fans spent their hard-earned dollars to travel to England and stand in front of the Beatles' homes or in front of Apple Records. It was a once in a lifetime experience.

The hours in front of the Park Lane were spent sharing stories. Linda proved to be a master storyteller, sharing her encounters with Paul in New York, London and Scotland. Her animated method of storytelling was entertaining and was supplemented by stories about George and Pattie, Ringo and Maureen, but little about John and Yoko.

We heard conflicting stories about why John was not at the concert. Originally, we were told he was joining George and Ringo on stage. When we were at the office on Friday, the Assistant Director, Patti, got a phone call to go to the hotel and help Yoko pack. Someone said John had left New York that morning without Yoko and no one knew why. Several stories circulated at the hotel. The only clue we got was that John supposedly said he didn't like the people at the hotel. From that point, people came up with other stories, such as he didn't like the service, or he left because Paul came in to town, or because Yoko embarrassed him in front of everyone. One ridiculous story came from one of the girls in a group called the Apple Scruffs. She claimed she spoke to Phil Spector who told her someone named Ben stole many of John and George's personal items, including clothing, and had skipped town and that was why John left. The story that ended up having the most weight was that John had argued with George because George didn't want Yoko on stage and John did. Regardless of why he left, the fact was he wasn't there and it was quite a disappointment.

Various stories about Paul were circulating as well. Some said he came alone and was staying at another hotel, but that did not prove to be true. We swallowed almost any and every rumor we heard because they all came from "reliable" sources—i.e. the chauffeurs, various members of their party and even Mal Evans who told Linda Woods that there would be a surprise at the concert. We took this to mean more than two of the Beatles would be there. Obviously, Bob Dylan was the surprise although from everyone's reaction, I could have sworn everyone knew about his appearance beforehand.

George and Ringo came out of the hotel around 7:30 that evening. The crowd was pretty large by then and I resented the presence of some come-lately fans that hadn't sweated it out as we had since early that morning. The limos pulled up to the hotel and George and Ringo literally flew out the door and into the car and drove off. I was pushed aside as the crowd ran after the car, screaming "George" and pounding on the doors. All I got was about a five-second glimpse from afar. That is what all those years of devotion led to—a brief glimpse, nothing more.

I stood alone on that sidewalk—alone, yet surrounded by so many people. The years flashed across my mind—starting the club in eighth grade, the friends I had lost and gained, the concerts, and the stories I so earnestly believed. The impact of being so close, yet so far, shook me more than anything else. And it wasn't even Paul I had seen—just a blurred vision of George and Ringo dashing into the backseat of a limo.

An unexpected feeling of absolute despondency came over me. I'm sick, I kept thinking. *This* is sick, but I couldn't help the way I felt. My dignity had been destroyed, and I had the urge to run as far from the Park Lane as I could get. Suddenly, I realized that I was indeed running. I left everyone there—not caring what happened to them or what was going to happen to me. I kept thinking I had to get out of New York, away from those kids and the ugliness of the groupie scene.

I slowed down as I walked toward our hotel, trying to keep from crying, trying to understand why I was even there and trying to patch my battered ego and regain my composure. That walk back to the hotel seemed like an eternity.

That night I decided to give up my position as National Chapter Director because it no longer meant anything to me. In truth, it meant absolutely nothing to anyone else as well. I also decided to disband the Paul chapter instead of giving it to the girl I had chosen as my successor. Disbanding was the one thing the national fan club did not want me to do. Out of bitterness I was willing to do everything and anything that was in opposition to what they wanted. I intended to leave New York and not bother to stay for the concert. I tried to get a flight out that evening, but since I was flying standby there was nothing available.

Linda called that night and I told her how I felt. For the first time, someone was genuinely interested in my welfare, not about the effect any decision I made would have on the club. She convinced me to stay, only because she promised to come and talk to me the next day. I trusted her judgment. She had nothing to lose if I left town and like me, she didn't give a damn about how the national club would react.

In the light of day you see things differently. Linda came to the hotel and so did Carol and Julie, area secretaries for New Jersey and Pennsylvania, respectively. I had wanted to talk to Linda alone, because there was so much to say to her that I thought only she could comprehend, but because of mixed company, the conversation took a different turn. It wasn't until I left the hotel with Linda, Carol and Julie that we really talked about the fan club and what could be done to salvage things.

We went to Madison Square Garden that afternoon just to hang around and see what was happening. It looked like a gathering at Woodstock. While thousands poured into the Garden for the afternoon concert, an equal number roamed around begging for tickets. Photos and lithographs of John and Yoko were being sold and people were handing out Bangladesh buttons in exchange for a donation. Others were asking you to sign petitions to have the U.S. government get involved in the Bangladesh crisis. They were even selling "WE STILL LOVE THE BEATLES" pennants, probably taken out of storage from the 1966 concerts.

I became bored and returned to the hotel. Later, while I was getting ready to go to the concert, Laura called and I somehow mustered up enough courage—perhaps acting out of anger or disappointment or humiliation or whatever—to tell her how I felt. I thought that Laura, having started as a fan and worked her way up in the ranks, would sympathize and understand and offer something to hold on to—a lick of an ice cream cone I saw melting away rapidly. She insisted quite vehemently that she did all she could for us—for all the area secretaries and chapter presidents who called her. She said she had called every day about those seats, that she knew we deserved them more than anyone else. She said that the hard-core truth was that Allen Klein and everyone else on the 41st floor didn't give a damn about the club or the people in it. Rusty and Sandi had hinted at this before. Laura told me that the fan club, more or less, revolved on its own. While they had to have everything approved upstairs, for the most part they could do what they wanted just as long as they left everyone else alone. She told me that if she became a pest about obtaining tickets for us, the club would have encountered serious trouble because management would become so fed up with her that they would go so far as to disband the club and fire the staff. I didn't want that to happen to her, but I told her I didn't understand the logic of their excuses. I had to call a spade a spade, and I told her I didn't believe the bit about Senator Kennedy getting turned down and yet she and her boyfriend were able to attend. How, I asked Laura, were we to get through to them? When you have to stand in front of a hotel and see groupies get into Apple's limos, you begin to wonder—do you have to go *that* far to get close? Do we have to belittle ourselves in order to get into the hotel or get a ticket to a concert?

Despite this unpleasantness, when I think back, I consider myself fortunate to have been there in the first place. The Concert for Bangladesh was hailed as the first benefit concert of its kind that brought together major artists of the day who were working together for a common humanitarian cause. Since then, concerts of this type—using music to serve a higher cause—have become commonplace. None of us realized we were witnessing a historic first, or how that concert set the standard for future humanitarian performances.

Ticket Stub to the Bangla Desh concert

Both concerts were sold out, and we were privileged to be able to see some of the top names in music at that time at the evening concert. In addition to George and Ringo, performers included Eric Clapton, Bob Dylan, Billy Preston, Leon Russell, and Ravi Shankar. The audience did not consist of Beatle fans as we had expected. The shove-it-in-your face pot-smoking crowd who attended was ill behaved. I was far from being in my comfort zone. I didn't smoke, drink, or do drugs, and I dressed conservatively. Clearly, I was the freak in this crowd.

From our vantage point at the side of the stage, we could stare down easily at the front rows where Apple employees were seated. I tried to put that out of my mind and be grateful for just being there.

When George and Ringo were on stage, you felt that same electricity in the air as at the Beatles concerts and it had quite an emotional impact on me after all I had been through the previous day. During the concert, I knew I couldn't just give up on everything. I was a fan in the deepest possible sense and that is what I would always be.

I admit, I had a difficult time relating to music other than Beatles music. I apparently wasn't the only one. *In We're Going to See the Beatles!,* author Garry Berman quotes a Beatle fan as saying: "George's Bangladesh concert was kind of like a mini–Beatle concert, a little quieter, because you didn't have all of them onstage. I think a lot of people were trying to pretend that they were okay with Ravi Shankar's music. I wasn't one to pretend it; it bored me."

When the concert ended, we ran out of the Garden in the hope of making it back to the Park Lane to see Ringo and George when they arrived. We couldn't get a taxi and finally decided to pile in Eileen's car and drive there. We missed seeing them by five minutes. My head was pounding by then, but everyone insisted we stand in front of the hotel because Ringo and George would be leaving to attend a party.

Ringo and Maureen leaving the Park Lane Hotel

After what seemed like an endless wait, Ringo and Maureen came down, hand-in-hand, and got into the limo and drove off. George and Pattie had meanwhile gotten into the car from the other entrance, along with George's dad who was really a wonderful person and so great to the fans. Once they left, I hoped no one would suggest we wait until they returned. I felt as though I were going to faint. Luckily everyone piled back into the car and returned to the hotel.

On the flight back to Chicago the next day, I thought about the parasites and exploiters who lived off the Beatles. I thought about the Beatles' inner circle and realized I did not belong there. My fantasy about believing that hard work, devotion, and skill would bring me to their attention, was just that—a fantasy. I thought, good Lord Joanne, even if they did acknowledge you, would you accept them for who they really are rather than the image you have created in your mind of who you think they should be or could be? The answer was no.

Laura had told me that the only way for the powers that be to recognize anyone in the fan club would be if everyone quit and she was forced to hire twelve new people to do the work. Quit? A strike would be even better, I thought. We didn't want to challenge the fan club or to betray the Beatles. We wanted to be heard. We wanted to be treated as people, not as fools who, because of our distance from New York, would never know what was really going on. Apple Corps was evolving into something we thought the Beatles were against.

I remembered a quote from John: "As I told *Rolling Stone*, it's the same people who have the power, the class system didn't change one little bit. Of course, there are a lot of people walking around with long hair now and some trendy middle-class kids in pretty clothes, but nothing changed except that we all dressed up a bit, leaving the same bastards running everything."

I came to the conclusion that the only people who weren't exploiting the Beatles were the fans. If you took one person out of the national fan club office and asked them to set up a Beatles-related organization and not get paid, it would never happen. Why then, I wondered, if no one cared, if you even were to work yourself up to a fancy title like National Chapter Director and get a check from Apple each month, you are told in no uncertain terms that as far as the organization is concerned, you are no better than a fan off the street. So why continue this farce? For the Beatles? Did they even care?

In my heart of hearts I realized that there was no reason for the fan clubs to stay with Apple. Independent clubs were just as good as chapters and all the reasons to be chapters and conform to Apple's rule, were one-sided and not essential to our survival. We had succeeded with our clubs long before we were put under their thumb. Who was to say we couldn't do it again?

In many ways, I felt betrayed. There had been nothing I would not have done for everyone at headquarters: No amount I wouldn't spend; no bending I wouldn't do to please them. When they said—don't print your personal opinions in your newsletter—I swallowed my pride and withheld my take on what was happening. When they said, don't mention Cynthia or Jane anymore, I understood and didn't. I played their game for years, but now I felt it was getting too ridiculous. I hated the system, and I hated what was being done to those of us who worked so hard for nothing.

Looking back, I realize all this whining about wanting recognition was all ego-based and part of my own karmic issue of needing outside validation. It would take me many years to understand that devoting yourself to something you deeply believe in without any expectation of reward or recognition, is a form of unconditional love. I had not yet been introduced to that concept so I tended to focus on the lack I felt rather than the fulfillment.

So it was that I decided to withdraw my services completely from the national club, not only as National Chapter Director, but also as president of Paul's chapter. I hoped others would follow my lead. This is where I learned about the power of thought because it didn't take very long for me to get my wish. Little did I know that events were unfolding that would fast forward the demise of all the fan clubs and disprove my contention that the Beatles would not become personally involved in the fate of the fan clubs.

It started with a letter Paul wrote to The Official Beatles Fan Club members in England in late August. Sara Schmidt writes: "He informed them that he had appreciated the support over the years, but it was time for him to withdraw from The Official Beatles Fan Club. He wrote, 'I don't want to be involved with anything that continues the illusion that there is such a thing as The Beatles.'" Sara goes on to write that in the United States, things were not so cut-and-dried. "Paul hadn't sent a letter to New York City, and he had never specified whether his request was only to the British Club or all clubs. That left confusion about the club's direction. Joanne Maggio, president of The Official Paul McCartney Chapter, was particularly confused. She was prepared to hand the club over to a fan in Brooklyn named Phyllis. Joanne wanted to focus her efforts on the official fan club. Then she heard about Paul's announcement, putting her club in limbo. "If OBFC remains for the Beatles, then the Paul chapter will have to either go independent or disband," she informed club members. They'd have to hope for the best while waiting on Allen Klein and Apple to tell them what to do. In the meantime Joanne promised she'd "continue giving you what you deserve and try to maintain chapter relationships as if nothing were happening."

And that's exactly what I did. My September 1971 newsletter contained news of the birth of Stella McCartney as well as comments about Paul's letter to the English Beatles Fan Club stating that he wished to no longer be a part of anything concerning the "Beatles." As a result, we had received a letter from the national club in New York saying that as of October 1, the so-called Official Beatles Fan Club would no longer exist, but was being reformed as the Apple Tree. The newly named club would still provide news, photos, etc. of the four individual guys as Apple artists, not as the Beatles. The club would also be incorporating other artists who had signed with Apple Records. We were told that any chapter name containing the word "Beatles" had to be changed, which was the only way they could get around Paul's desire to withdraw from the fan club completely. While he said he was no longer a Beatle, he was still recording on the Apple label, so I was allowed to maintain my chapter for him. There was one stipulation. The chapter had to be for both Paul and Linda because they were *both* Apple recording artists. I could not envision heading a chapter devoted to the two of them. Our membership had become so divided that I knew it was a no-win situation and that things would never get any better. I decided enough was enough. I announced in that newsletter that I would give the Paul chapter to someone who loved both Paul and Linda, had the patience, money, and time to spend on it that I no longer had. My time was drawing near an end. I just had a little housekeeping to do.

The October-November newsletter was a continuation of airing the controversy stoked by the pro and anti-Linda factions. I tried to remain unbiased and printed an even number of pro and con letters but it was clear, the level of animosity was heating up. I hoped I could get out of this mess without further emotional scarring.

Then fate took over and finally ended it for me—not with a whimper, but with a bang. In December 1971,

Laura phoned to say she had been called into Allen Klein's office. On Klein's desk was a copy of the George Harrison chapter's newsletter, George Gernal, which long had been considered one of the best newsletters among the fan clubs. Klein asked Laura about Pat Kinzer, the president of that chapter. He said George read the Gernal and reportedly called it "garbage." He supposedly disclaimed his own chapter and the entire fan club and contacted someone at Apple in London who contacted Klein to report George's angst over the Gernal. Klein did not say specifically what George did not like, but Laura surmised that it was probably something as simple as the mere concept of a "fan club." No further explanation was given and despite careful reading by Laura, she was unable to see what George found so objectionable. Neither could anyone else.

Klein disavowed any knowledge of the existence of chapters, saying he believed they had been disbanded years earlier when Ringo became incensed over a newsletter sent to him by his fan club. I was relieved that I never had the nerve to send Paul a copy of any of our newsletters, as undoubtedly we would have suffered the same fate.

Klein ordered a memo from Laura on the status of the fan club and its chapters. At the time of her first call, she was sure the chapters would be disbanded but the national fan club would remain and probably undergo drastic reorganization at the most. It turned out to be much worse than that.

Chapter Six

1972: And In The End . . .

1972

A few days later, Laura called to give me the news that the entire fan club had been dissolved. It seems that George did not let the matter rest (or Klein didn't) and was insistent upon action. The only way Klein could promise that the situation would not repeat itself was to dissolve the entire fan club. Laura's memo said the national club had dwindled to 4,200 members and Klein did not feel this warranted continuation of the club under any circumstances. George, now joined by Ringo, called a meeting at Apple in London and Freda Kelly, head of the English fan club, was asked to come.

At the time of her call, Laura said that there was a good chance the club in England would fold as well. When I asked her what we could do, she kept repeating, "I don't care." She said we had been heading in this direction for several months now. Her only concern at that moment was whether she would still have a job, which they had assured her she would. I asked her when and how she was going to handle the announcement. She told me that she didn't think it was a good idea to mention the George Gernal because she feared people would automatically assume that Pat Kinzer was the cause of the dissolution of not only the chapters but also the entire fan club. Yet on January 17, 1972, she sent the following letter to all chapter presidents and area secretaries:

> As you are all so aware, the Beatles are no longer recording as a group. Since it was the intention of the club when it was formed that it be a Beatles Fan Club, the management of Apple, at this time, feel it is unfair to keep the club active on this basis. Therefore, as of this date, the club, both in the United States and England, is being dissolved. All I can say is that I am, of course, very disappointed and even shocked, that this club must come to an end. I truly hoped that as the Apple Tree we had a long future.
>
> I would like to explain what has pulled the trigger. One of our FINEST chapters sent out a newsletter, which did not agree with John, George or Ringo. They all feel that they do not want news, such as this newsletter contained, being sent out. At some later date, if it is possible to form a different kind of club, we hope that you will be willing to help us out in some way.

I would like to take this opportunity to thank each and every one of you for all the help you have given to the club. I hope to continue working for Apple, and therefore would still love to hear from you. Best wishes in all your future endeavors. Thanks again. Love Laura.

I was furious. Laura had ordered me to keep quiet about this. No one was to know, and I wasn't to make any plans as to our future. I begged her to call Pat and at least give her a heads up, but she refused. I remained quiet, yet found out later that she shared the news with others who called asking what was going on. I was sorry I didn't get out our "truth" letter before she made her announcement.

Ironically, of all the Beatle club presidents, Pat Kinzer had been closest to George and his family. Pat considered herself fortunate to be in such a close relationship to the Harrison family and that is why I knew this had to be a devastating blow to her. None of us saw it coming. George was the last of the Beatles we ever expected to do something like this, especially when in that same Gernal that George called "garbage," Pat mentioned the three charities the club went all out for—the Bangladesh Fund, the foster child in Thailand, and above all, the Louise Harrison Cancer Fund. He may not have liked some of the content, but the fact remained, the chapter newsletter was not written for the Beatles to read. There was no way it could focus on George's eastern philosophies or Ravi Shankar's music—if that's what he wanted—and still hold on to the demographics of the younger members.

We speculated that what bothered George was that the Gernal had published portions of an interview in the February issue of *Cosmopolitan* that discussed Pattie and his personal life in a somewhat negative way. Or maybe he was just fed up by everything that was transpiring around him where the Beatles were concerned. I could understand if he did not approve of the concept of a "fan club," but I didn't think he, nor anyone else, understood how many people would be hurt by the demise of the fan club. Closing it was a slap in the face to all fans, but an even bigger slap in the face to Pat who clearly was blindsided.

Writing in her book, *Do You Promise Not to Tell: The Final Story of the Official George Harrison Fan Club,* Pat shared the depths of her emotional pain at this turn of events:

> I could not understand for the life of me WHY someone I knew, whose family I adore (and I know they liked me back), whom I had worked so very hard for, for eight years, would do something so terrible to me. I had never done a thing to him. I loved him. WHY or WHAT would make him do this? All I heard were rumors of why he did this—some said it was that article about George and Pattie adopting children; some said it was because George didn't like me intruding into private things, particularly the death of

his mother. The reason his father all of a sudden took off for Los Angeles right before he was to meet me in England to go to his wife's grave was supposedly because George got wind of the whole thing and didn't want his father subjected to it. When it came to his mother's death, George was very possessive of the whole thing.

Upset was not a strong enough word to describe my feelings. Betrayed, insulted, humiliated, spit on, trashed, furious are appropriate words that come to mind. When I found out the truth, I cried and cried and cried. No one could console me. Even my mother cried. The Harrisons had become part of our family. The only thing left for me to do was inform my fan club members, and I wrote a heart-wrenching letter to them, telling them everything that happened.

After mailing out her last newsletter, Pat went home and cried some more.

I wrote letters to George, begging him to let me know WHY he did this to me. I wrote letters to Laura Cayne, asking her why she hadn't told me this herself. I wrote letters to George's father . . . I wrote to Freda Kelly, begging for some sort of explanation. Freda responded, telling me that indeed my newsletter really caused all this, but that she had been planning to stop the fan club anyway . . . She told me not to blame myself and to remember that George is human and does lose his temper sometimes, but deep down he is nice.

With the announcement of the club's demise, I felt strangely liberated and decided to share everything that had gone on in August when I visited Apple headquarters for the last time. Laura told me that if I printed the article revealing what I saw and heard, she'd consider it my resignation and the resignation of anyone in the club who dared to agree with me. She would write a rebuttal, slamming me and anything I said, even if it were true (which it was). But with orders to disband, I had nothing to lose. I printed the saga of my experience in New York and finally said what I had thought all along—that the excuses to keep us as chapters of the national club had been a farce for years. I was glad we were out on our own now. And then I said goodbye.

Giving up the chapter was the hardest thing I ever had to do. It took me nearly two years to work up to that decision, and when I finally publicly said I was leaving, I felt as if a great weight had been lifted. My father was glad it was over, saying I had finally "grown up." All I knew was that something had shifted after July 31st when I saw George at the Park Lane. It was then I realized it was time to wake

January 1972 Newsletter

up. The decision I made in New York was irrevocable. I wouldn't turn back or change my mind.

Now when I look back on those eight years, I can clearly see the pros and cons and how they would relate to my later life. During the Beatles years, I chose to neglect many things in my personal life and put myself in a position where I was an easy target. Every life reaches a fork in the road, where one path will take you to one destination and the other someplace else. Had I not done the fan club, I could have put much more of myself into my studies. I could have gotten involved in worthwhile volunteer activities. I could have saved money and made good use of it. I could have made real and lasting friends instead of coupling up with people I later identified as users and abusers.

Being a fan club president wasn't as easy as being a fan. It was a 24-hour, seven-day a week, 12 month a year job. It wasn't an occasional buying of a record or attending a movie or a party. You had to deal with the haters. As Rusty once told me: "A chapter president works for herself, Jo, not for the Beatles." It was true. I did what I did because I wanted to do it. I said it was for the Beatles, but it was for me. I continuously made excuses to keep it going. Once in a while, some angel would write and say she appreciated what I did, but most other times I had to deal with deranged fans calling me, demanding I tell Paul they loved him.

I stood in front of the Park Lane Hotel for nearly ten hours to catch a glimpse of one of the Beatles. I stood there feeling cheap and humiliated. I had worked hard over the years but there I was, indistinguishable from the teenyboppers who surrounded me. I realized how bitter I had become—bitter more at myself for being so foolish and staying with it for so long. As my upbringing taught me to look at life as the glass half-empty rather than half-full,

I slid into what I perceived to be the negative energy of the experience, rather than focus on the good things that happened during my tenure. I had to work at looking at it from a positive perspective.

And so that's what I did. I thought about everything I could put in the plus column of those eight years. In my final newsletter, I acknowledged the truly wonderful people who came into my life and touched my heart in ways that were too numerous to mention. Those years as a Beatles fan club president aided me in coming out of my shell. I developed qualities of leadership, understood the value of money and the satisfaction of hard work and conflict resolution. I learned to develop photos, write and produce newsletters, create a data base, handle finances and mass mailings. I began to look deeper into the meaning of life. I had a lot ahead of me. It was time to move on, to get into bigger and better things.

On February 7, 1972, the eighth anniversary of starting the fan club, I turned the Paul chapter over to Sarah Nolte who lived in Indianapolis. I was confident Sarah would take it to the next level. Sher Miller, my friend from New York, was also coming on board as vice president. With that team, I was certain the transition would go smoothly.

Sarah intended to keep the Paul chapter independent and the other clubs were going to try to remain together. I promised to stay involved somehow, although once I gave the club to Sarah, I never looked back. I ended my farewell newsletter with a poem by Wilbur D. Nesbit:

All to myself I think of you,
Think of the things we used to do,
Think of the things we used to say,
Think of each happy bygone day.
Sometimes I sigh
And sometimes I smile
But I keep each olden,
Golden while
All to myself.

After I made the announcement and Sarah came to Chicago to collect all the materials I had accumulated over the years, a strange silence descended over my Bridgeport home. No more bundles of mail to open and answer every day. No more phone calls. No more photo developing. No more work that kept me occupied all night. I was going cold turkey. The silence was deafening and at times I didn't know what I would do.

What I would soon find out was that 1972 would be my year of liberation. It may have been the end of the Beatlemania era in my life, but it also signaled the beginning of something entirely new—something I could never have envisioned possible. It was the end of my time in Bridgeport, as my parents had a new home built in the Chicago suburb of Downers Grove. But it also was the beginning of a long, Rip Van Winkle type of sleep. During that time, I did exactly what Joshua M. Greene describes in *Here Comes the Sun*: "By the mid-seventies, the young people who helped make George Harrison a superstar had become adults. Sixties-era protesters went home to find jobs and have families."

I finished college, got a job, got married, bought a house in the suburbs and started a family. For all intents and purposes, I slipped into a deep sleep in a cocoon of my own making and did not emerge until the big spiritual wake-up call initiated by Shirley MacLaine in January 1987.

Chapter Seven

Think For Yourself: The Spiritual Impact of the Beatles On Other Fans

While I knew how the Beatles made their mark on my spiritual quest, I wondered if the same thing happened to other fans. I cast a net through Facebook and my newsletter database to search for men and women who, like me, followed a spiritual path because of the influence of the Beatles.

The average age of those who responded to my questionnaire was seventy, so I knew I was working with the "original" fans who were in their early teens when the Beatles arrived on the scene in 1964. Out of the ten who filled out my questionnaire, I was surprised that only three had seen them in person. One of those was someone who later would become instrumental in my own spiritual growth.

How I met Nan is a story in synchronicity at work. On November 9, 2000, long before we met, I was involved in a near-fatal car crash. Prior to this, I was very active in my metaphysical studies as a member of Edgar Cayce's A.R.E. and director of my own past-life research organization.

Within days of the accident, I noticed an abrupt change in my attitude. I became less and less interested in spiritual topics until they no longer interested me at all. I started to back away from my like-minded friends, disbanded my past-life organization, and did not renew my membership in the A.R.E. I gave away most of my metaphysical library and began to live a more mainstream life.

This went on for three years until the anniversary of the car accident—November 9, 2003. When I awoke that morning, I was "back" to the person I had been three years earlier. My spiritual interests were front and center, as if they never left. What had left, however, were my friends, my past-life organization and my library of treasured research materials. For the next three years, I tried to put everything back together again, to no avail. Then I switched tactics and decided to search for answers to explain what happened to me.

My father passed away in 2006, leaving me a small inheritance. I had long wanted to get my Masters Degree, but did not know what to major in, or how I could afford a graduate degree. I also thought I was getting a bit old to pursue this, feeling inadequate to compete with younger students. When I discovered that A.R.E. offered a Masters in Transpersonal Studies degree through its school, Atlantic University, I jumped at the chance to enroll. I had once heard someone say that Edgar Cayce saved her life. I was so despondent at this point that I thought why not see if Edgar would do the same for me. This was the wisest choice I ever made as I was slowly reintroduced to the esoteric studies I had abandoned years before. As a bonus, this experience gave me the answer as to why I had lost interest in spirituality after the accident.

The last year of my studies, I had to take some electives and chose to do one on Near Death Experience (NDE). A required reading was *Coming Back to Life: Examining the After-Effects of the Near-Death Experience* (NDE), by PMH Atwater. I never considered the experience I had at my auto accident as an NDE because I did not lose consciousness. Fortunate for me, PMH went to the same Unity Church that I attended and we knew each other. One Sunday, I approached her and told her about my experience. She asked me if I thought I was going to die at the moment of impact and I said yes, I did. According to her, when that thought occurred, my soul may have shot out of my body for a brief moment, thus giving me the NDE.

In Atwater's book, she described one of the symptoms of an NDE as losing all interest in the life you led prior to the near-death experience. That was it! So not only did my studies at Atlantic University answer a question I had been asking for nine years, but it also increased my overall confidence thanks to the positive responses I received about my essays from my course mentors. I became more actively involved with the A.R.E. again and began focusing my attention in the area of reincarnation research and therapy. The rest, as they say, is history.

When I met Nan, she and her husband Carlos, headed up Atlantic University. I don't know how common it was for students to become friends with the school directors, but somehow, we connected. When we got together for dinner during one of my visits to Virginia Beach, I was surprised at just how much we had in common. Not only were we both from the Chicago area, but we were both avid Beatles fans. It seemed we were operating in the same circle, and yet our paths never crossed during those early Beatle days.

"I helped a lot with the local newsletters in a minor way (stuffing envelopes)," she told me. "My three friends and I were crazy about the Beatles as were most of the people I knew in grade school and high school. I never missed a movie, saw both *Hard Day's Night* and *Help* a dozen or so times."

Nan and I both attended the Beatles concert at Comiskey Park and like me, she described it as "an amazing experience." After that concert, her room began to fill up with Beatles posters. Like me, Nan had to feed her Beatle appetite in unique ways:

> I spent time at a friend's house when they were first in Chicago in 1964. Neither of us were allowed to go by our parents. And I had been listening to their music through a friend in Scotland who had seen them in person a year or so before. Saw all the televised stuff in their

first visit to the US. Bought all the albums as
they came out. It was just a heightening of my
interest in them, read a lot, did at least a dozen
scrapbooks of articles of our poems and stories
and everything I found in the newspapers or in
the newsletters and in the teen magazines. Their
interest in rock and roll and their musical pref-
erences impacted on mine from the beginning.
They were just my world at the beginning.

In the course of my reaching out to my Beatle fan
contemporaries, I was not surprised to hear so many share
Nan's feeling that the Beatles "were just my world from
the beginning."

"I did hang onto every word when I first became a
Beatles fan," said Deborah, a Beatles fan from the age of
fourteen, "so something surely touched me subconsciously.
Otherwise, I don't think I would still be a fan."

One of those who responded to my questionnaire
was Julie. We were both students at the all-girls St. Barbara
High School in Chicago. Despite being close friends at the
time, Julie was not a part of my fan club so we did not have
many of the same Beatle experiences. "I never joined a
Beatles fan club, nor any other club or group, because that
took commitment," she admits. "I preferred the flexibility
of aligning myself with a wide range of groups or movements or philosophies."

Julie did not see the Beatles in concert, but that isn't to say she didn't "see" them. She was there when their limos drove west down 43rd Street @ Francisco, going from the International Amphitheater to Midway Airport after that evening's concert.

"How can I brag with such outrageous confidence that we saw their limos go by?" Julie asks. "Easy. It was after 10:30 p.m. on a weekday night. We were still outside playing street volleyball. Nobody rode in a limo in our neighborhood back then. The DJs on WLS and WCFL said that the Beatles had just wrapped up their show shortly before that." Julie's response at seeing the motorcade? "Shock and awe as we collectively realized what we were witnessing," she says.

As I alluded to earlier, one of the questions I grappled with, in terms of understanding my metaphysical career, was whether having grown up Catholic made me more susceptible to being influenced by something that was the antithesis of Catholic dogma—something like reincarnation. I learned other Catholic teens felt the same way.

Rich, who discovered the Beatles when he was sixteen, was one of them. Like me, he felt as though he was born with the question "why?" and like me, no answers came from the authorities:

> Having been raised Catholic and following the faith, although never really digging it, I found myself as an early teen questioning many of the dogmas and policies of the church. Catholicism

never really made sense to me, but I did what I was told and taught until I could reason for myself. I didn't have the guts to say so or to not follow and go along. My mother's family would not have taken kindly to doing so. Therefore, I went along, genuflected, took the host, kneeled and looked like I was praying, all the while singing the Beatles songs in my head. I really got good at it. I didn't realize at the time the Beatles came along, but I was already a recovering Catholic. I just didn't have the meetings to go to for support. Except for going through the motions, I was not a practicing Catholic any longer. I was a seeker in search of my higher-self.

Julie, who with me and our fellow classmates, were subjected to a rather rigid view of Catholicism from the nuns and priests at St. Barbara High School, had the benefit of what she called "an incredibly open-minded" mother, "quite a renaissance woman herself" who "didn't stop me from learning more about philosophies and cultures, so, I never felt religious constraints." While Julie's grandmother thought Julie was going to become a Hindu because of the company she kept and the music she listened to, her father decided it was just a phase she was going through. Julie adds that she continued to attend church and was a practicing Catholic while she was living at home and "grooving" to Eastern philosophy. After marrying and leaving home, she stopped attending services and leaned more toward Eastern philosophies. "I tried applying a Buddhist mind-set but couldn't reconcile it with my inner feistiness," she admits. "I was a firm adherent to the concept of reincarnation, but felt like I was going down a rabbit hole. In my mid-50s, I found myself being drawn back to Catholicism through a different lens."

Rich realized the Beatles were going down a more spiritual path when he was in the Navy in 1966:

> I had rejected religion a few years before but kept up the good face for my mother. I was sort of in limbo (so to speak) spiritually when *Revolver* and then *Sgt. Pepper* came out. "Tomorrow Never Knows" was the first blush for me as it opened the door to the esoteric aspect of spirituality, rather than the dogma of religion that had become so stagnant for me. I say 'opened the door' because I was raised traditional Catholic and thus had no real inkling of spirituality. Meditation was a word without meaning to me. When I made the connection of the word to "… turn off your mind, relax and float downstream …" it was like a huge "ah-ha" bubble over my head. Follow that up with "Within You and Without You," and I am now beginning to clamor for more insight and depth to the whole reality of spirituality. It wasn't until I got out of

the Navy and more freely exploring books and articles on the subject that more and more of it made sense. I was able then to find hidden meanings in so much of the music done by John and George.

When all of this happened, Rich felt a release from the weight of Catholicism: "It was a bit like the first skinny-dipping episode with a lovely young lady. A little apprehensive at first blush but quickly so freeing and opening up to the whole idea of being totally, fully and completely exposed to a person of the opposite sex. You dream of it but when it is right there it is like lightning bolts coursing through you. Just Wow!"

When Nan first realized the Beatles were going down a spiritual path, she was more than ready to join them:

I was ready because I was already unhappy with Catholicism, partly because of the widely changing attitude of one of the nuns who was a favorite teacher in high school. My first husband was Jewish. He also had found his way to spirituality through the Beatles and through hallucinogens. We bonded over having moved towards George Harrison more. We both felt that George was very serious and showed that in his life and music, especially more than the others. The Concert for Bangladesh was a big event in our relationship.

How did this shift in consciousness impact Nan's religious upbringing? She states:

> I got more and more disappointed with Catholicism and its autocratic anti-woman, anti-situational values stand. When I converted to Judaism, my ex-husband was a Reform Jew and that's how I was involved. We divorced by the time I moved to North Carolina, and Carlos (my husband until his passing in July 2021) had gone through the spiritual awakening to Eastern religions and philosophy through the Beatles as well although because he was younger, in a less direct way. His interest in consciousness and psychic phenomena was even more important in our bonding. But music, and Eastern religion and philosophy was important too. My dislike for institutional religions especially here in the states has never left me. Spirituality flows from within, I think, and it is much more important than the religions that grow up around it.

This reaction wasn't limited to recovering Catholics. Doug, who grew up in a fundamental Christian church, says: "The Beatles and other sources led me to a general spirituality and finding truth in all paths." Doug resonated to the spiritual message the Beatles provided that "there is more to life than the mundane things that I spend most of my time on, yet it's all part of the journey."

Deborah said she had a unique religious upbringing. "I was raised Baptist, and educated Catholic," she explains. "I was the only non-Catholic in the school." When she was six and in the first grade at a Catholic school, she remembered the nun's lesson on the journey of the soul:

> She said that when we die, the soul goes on but there is no such thing as reincarnation. Into my little six-year-old brain popped the thought as clear as a bell, *Oh yes there is!* So that's something I have always embraced. This caused a lot of confusion and as a result, I turned away from religion altogether. However, in my late twenties I began to study spirituality, and in the last essay of my Atlantic University MA degree, I was able to reconcile all of my religious education into a cohesive belief system that not only worked for me, but provided a lot of relief from the confusion. And once I saw that you were doing this study, and I really thought about it, I realized the impact the Beatles had, and still do, on my spirituality. I think we all owe them a great deal of gratitude for their music.

Jeannie was baptized in the Methodist Church and had a strict upbringing. Nonetheless, her parents gave her the room to explore her spirituality on her own terms. Jeannie noted: "I became interested in meditation, yoga and the lessons of the gurus. For some reason all that resonated with me. My parents were key to opening my interest in spirituality in that they would ask questions that were contradictory to traditional teachings." Jeannie says she went on to study Bahai. She went to the Kingdom Hall with Jehovah's Witnesses, Catholic churches, and then back to the Methodist church. After she divorced, she found Unity and that felt more like home to her.

For Jeannie, the first realization that the Beatles were going down a more spiritual path came around the time of the release of *Sgt. Pepper*, but she adds that when listening to "Strawberry Fields," she began to feel changes happening in the world: "I think the most inspirational for me was "Strawberry Fields Forever" … because nothing is real."

Susan, baptized a Lutheran but raised in the Presbyterian church, learned how to separate her personal beliefs from what she called "official Presbyterianism": "I don't openly share the 'controversial' parts of my belief with other members of the congregation, as it is, on the whole, a conservative group that would neither approve of nor accept my views on reincarnation. I tend to share my beliefs only with a small circle of close, accepting, like-minded friends."

Julie had the advantage of having a parent who was more open to this shift to spiritualism than others. Julie explains:

> My mom has always had a guilty interest in exploring Eastern philosophies and spirituality. Guilty because of her Catholic upbringing. She was a 'lite' adherent to astrology; when I was pretty young, she told me that she thought I was an Egyptian in a former life; when I was a teen, I told her that I somehow felt more connected to the African Savannah than to Egypt. As it turned out, we were both kind of right—I did a DNA test recently and found that my traceable maternal origins are in Sierra Leone, which occupies the extreme western edge of Africa's savanna biome . . . Anyway, this early exposure to Eastern philosophy, spirituality and lite occult, made it feel familiar-ish and not something I thought of doing out of rebellion. I read different classic texts (the Vedas, Upanishads, Bhagavad Gita), went to lectures, and immersed myself in the music and culture. I even took my mom, herself a classically trained opera singer interested in diverse musical genres, to Ravi Shankar concerts and to parties with my Indian friends. She's totally hooked on Bollywood movies, soaps and sitcoms.

Susan, a teacher with a bachelor's degree in English and a master's degree in library science, says: "It wasn't until after I retired and experienced several past-life journeys that I discovered I had been involved in teaching, writing, and libraries in more than one past life, so it isn't surprising that I was drawn to these same choices again. The Beatles weren't really influential in my career choice except for the fact that teaching had been my fallback plan in case I didn't meet and get the opportunity to work for them."

Jeannie adds that when the Beatles went to India to study, she became more and more interested in what they were doing:

> My resources were limited at the time and, although I often went to the library in Buffalo, I really didn't know where to begin looking for the things I was interested in. I would often check out albums of music from different cultures: from African to Indian and Asian. This led me to study different religions as well. I felt like doors were finally opening into a truer reality. Had the Beatles not opened the door I may have taken a slightly different route, but I'm sure it would have been much more subtle. I think as they influenced the world and as everything changed, so did I. I think the world needs another band or leader as influential as the Beatles to get it back on course.

Nan realized the Beatles were seeding spiritual enlightenment when they traveled to India and began talking about Indian music. "I started listening to Indian music, mainly sitar albums, and reading Patanjali and other Indian philosophers," she says. "I really resonated to their movement toward a spiritual path. That kind of thing led me to investigate Bahai and Buddhism, as well as other religions and philosophy. I was already interested in Edgar Cayce and psychic phenomena. I started meditating more because of the Beatles' ideas and experiences."

Julie's realization that the Beatles were heading down the path of spirituality came in 1966. "I kept up with their following the Maharishi, George's learning the sitar, and the seismic shift in the complexity and depth of their music and lyrics," she said.

Jeannie, whose career is in technology, says meditation has kept her sane. She traveled to Peru with Shamans and had experiences with ayahuasca: "The ceremonies led me to being freer in expressing myself through the different forms of art I play with. So although my career is one thing, my spiritual side balances my life out." Jeannie credits the Beatles for opening that spiritual door and making it okay for her to walk through:

> They showed me that because I was born and raised a certain way, there was more to life than what I knew. I realized I could do more, travel more, and live a more fulfilled life than what I

was shown growing up. I've had mystical experiences but I think that once the Beatles opened that door, I found it was okay to learn more and that my path through life could be different. I've had dreams and visions, and I even met my spirit guide in an ayahuasca trip. I saw how I was protected from forces that could possibly harm me. I learned how I wasn't alone. If I had not been influenced by the Beatles, fear would have continued to run my life.

I was intrigued that many of the fans I spoke to gravitated to Edgar Cayce's Association for Research and Enlightenment, the A.R.E., just as I did. I already spoke about Nan, who was the head of the A.R.E.'s Atlantic University. Joy also was interested in the A.R.E. A Beatle fan since the age of eleven when she saw them in person in Indianapolis—an event she still considers a peak experience—Joy also was raised Catholic and said she was deeply religious growing up but by eleven, was having doubts about some of the rules and the existence of hell: "Reincarnation was much fairer than the idea of heaven and hell. I was still in middle and high school so had no freedom to pursue a different path—but it was in my head. In my early twenties, I got involved in the A.R.E. Clinic and studying the Cayce readings and other metaphysical topics and teachers became my religion. I am more spiritually involved than ever."

Rich also became involved with the A.R.E. He says:

It wasn't until a couple of years after the breakup
that I found the enlightenment of Edgar Cayce
and the Association for Research and Enlightenment. Upon that discovery I found so much
more truth in the concepts of Love is God is
Love, and that 'All there is is Love.' Although I
am not thinking of the proper references at this
moment, there is much of the Cayce philosophy
that is written and sung about in the years prior
to my Cayce find.

I asked the group what aspect of the Beatles interest
in spirituality resonated to them. Nan says: "Exploring
and understanding Eastern religions, meditation and consciousness, and the global aspect of it. Also, that Eastern
religion seems to emerge from within, while Catholicism
and other western religions were imposed by communi-
ties. I'm sure there was a certain ignorance of the social
construction of Eastern religions in that perspective."

Nothing within this experience turned her off:

Consciousness and having values and practices
come from within and not be imposed from
outside is still important to me. Meditating
became something that I just couldn't sustain,
but my interest in Eastern religions and other

religions expanded when I worked at the first parapsychology laboratory I was at (in Durham, NC). The director of the lab was from Andrah Pradesh, and the most important theorists in the field were designing studies that referred to and evolved from an understanding of Patanjali's writings. The global sense of being was reinforced by the international members of our laboratory, and that never left me.

Julie agrees that nothing about the Beatles' spiritual exploration was a turn off for her. "I appreciated their sincerity in exploring this," she says. "It also was obvious that it wasn't embraced the same way by all four, and when it became less than foremost in their personal and professional lives, it was okay to keep moving on."

When asked if at any point she embraced spirituality in her choice of career, Nan says no, but quickly adds: "Unless studying psychic phenomena, being in an environment in which survival and reincarnation research was taken seriously and having colleagues who emphasized the fundamental importance of our entanglement with each other feels spiritual, can be pointed to as a choice of career that came out of the understanding."

Julie also leaned in the direction of a "yes" response, but only if spirituality encompassed environmentalism:

In 1989, the lightbulb went on about conservation, biodiversity, sustainability, natural resources, and being more than an advocate for nature, but a practitioner of ecological responsibility. Nineteen eighty-nine was my environmental awakening, which I see as a direct descendant of my spiritual endeavors, and I started taking classes, working in the field with early proponents, organizing others to help with ecological restoration projects, and generally absorbing all that I could. In 1990 I had a serious illness and told myself that if I survived, I was going to go into conservation as a career. I did, and I did.

Like others, Julie could see how the Beatles may have been indirectly influential in her career choice: "They profoundly raised Western culture's awareness of peace, love and rock and roll. I found peace in nature; I found people who loved making a positive difference in the world; and I hear music everywhere—crickets, frogs, trees (ever hear sap rising under the bark?), it's all sacred music."

Although everyone in my survey agreed that of all the Beatles, George was the most serious about following a spiritual path, he was not necessarily their favorite in the group. Nonetheless, it was George who shone a light on the spiritual aspect of life and that light was so bright, many could not resist following its illuminated path.

"George, indisputably," Julie answers. "I think John, a hugely layered personality with diverse interests, was drawn to mysticism and dabbling in Indian music, but ultimately had other things going on in his life that eventually caused a separation from those influences. George, on the other hand, found his philosophical and music center with these."

Rich agrees:

> He [George] went deep into spirituality without shame or reservation. When he found it, it was like he leapt forward and wanted to convince everyone about how wonderful the view was. John had the inclination to share insights into spirituality in a more subtle way, I think, that had a more political sense. Because George was so introspective and had deep insight into the spirituality of life on this planet, I always preferred him to the more brash John. George just seemed to live a more genuinely kind and considerate life which reflected his depth of soul.

Rich adds that as a result, he began to follow George more closely: "Before his spiritual awakening, his songs seemed superficial, but after his awakening they felt to have matured and dug deeper into his soul."

But George wasn't the only Beatle whose comments made an impact on the spiritual growth of their fans. When asked if he ever heard something in an interview that really spoke to him and moved him in a different direction, Doug gives that credit to Paul when he says: "This moment is important because it's all we really have." Living in the present moment is certainly one of the guideposts along a spiritual path.

With a few exceptions, however, it was George's embracing a spiritual lifetime that had a strong hold on fans who were intrigued with the message he was sharing. That is not to say that it was easy, even for the staunchest Beatle-maniac, to remain with the group when it came to certain aspects of their lifestyle.

Gordon, who was around fourteen when he discovered the Beatles, says: "They were not what I would call role models, but they certainly did exemplify something else for me . . . those times were turbulent along with the Vietnam war . . . anti-war protesting, culminating in Kent State and Altamont . . . I think basically freed me up to step away from the things and choices from my own upbringing and allowed me to leave them behind to pursue my own search for meaning."

"I think the drugs would be the one thing that scared me at that time," says Jeannie. "I wasn't ready for the kinds of experiences some drugs offer, and I was still quite innocent."

Lisa says that the mere fact that this spiritual journey took them out of the limelight for a while was a turn off for her: "I was too young to understand it all. I honestly was concerned that they were someplace doing drugs and hallucinating."

Drugs were the biggest issue for many fans. Deborah states outright that their use of drugs turned her off. Susan, who was thirteen when the Beatles came on the scene, echoed that sentiment:

> I wasn't happy with the Beatles' decision to experiment with drugs, particularly LSD, although I realize that their drug usage probably was initially fueled by curiosity, along with a desire to find inner peace and to experience something that was missing in their lives, even though they may not have realized it at the time. I was also suspicious of the Maharishi's ulterior motives—was he truly interested in the spiritual development of the Beatles and other celebrities who were coming to him or was he more interested in achieving fame for himself?

When asked what aspect of this time in the Beatles' lives turned him off the most, Doug answers: "The fighting. Even spiritually advanced people have egos."

Several fans mention John's comment about Jesus as a memorable event. One fan cited it as her biggest turn off. "I wasn't into Jesus then, but it seemed arrogant," writes Joy.

Susan references this interview as well. When asked if she ever heard any of the Beatles say anything in an interview that really spoke to her or moved her in a different direction, she cites John's remark about the Beatles being more popular than Jesus. "What a controversy that remark provoked!" she says, adding:

> At the time, I was much more appalled by the public outcry than I was by John's words, which had been taken out of context. Radio stations decided to ban Beatles' records, 'fans' burned their albums, and Robert Fleming, one of Pennsylvania's state senators at the time, proposed prohibiting the Beatles from appearing or performing anywhere in the state. I wrote a Letter to the Editor, published in the *Pittsburgh Post-Gazette* on August 13, 1966, defending John and the 'boys,' as I called them then. I never considered John's statement blasphemous or an affront to my religious beliefs. By the time I was nine or ten, several years before the Beatles became a major part of my life, I already had begun to question and look a little outside the box of mainstream religion, and by my late teens, I had ventured far beyond its edges.

Lisa also got caught up in the controversy over John's statement: "That got me thinking about their power to influence in a huge way, and all that backlash from it showed me how people operate out of fear."

Julie says she was saddened by John having to explain what he meant: "It was the sixties, and I knew that America was racially prejudiced, but because my folks and immediate circle of family and friends were so, well, liberal, it never occurred to me that there could be such a religious backlash. In a sense, what he said made it even easier for me to want to explore different religious/philosophical options. It was honest curiosity rather than rebellion."

Joy says while the Beatles were not immediately influential in her choice of a spiritual career path, once she got to her early twenties, she was drawn to embrace spirituality more and more: "I had been wanting to be involved in the Cayce work and this seemed to be my life path." She felt this sense of spirituality most once she began working at the A.R.E. Clinic, "It was a cause and a religion of sorts, and a spiritual community. Now my writing and volunteer work with the A.R.E. certainly has a spiritual basis."

The most visible symbol of the Beatles' exploration of spirituality came when they ventured to India. That wasn't something I resonated to, and I wondered how other fans felt about it. Most knew nothing about Transcendental Meditation, nor did they follow it after the Beatles spent time with the Maharishi. Susan says:

> I was 17 when the Beatles became involved with the Maharishi's teachings and George, in particular, began to delve more deeply into Eastern philosophy and religion. At this point,

I was beginning to realize that even though the world's various religions might approach things differently, their ultimate goal—reunion with God—was the same. Quite honestly, I was not impressed by the Maharishi at the time. I knew little about Transcendental Meditation and saw the Maharishi as a bit of a con man, willing to use the Beatles as his own ticket to fame.

Reflecting on the involvement the Beatles had with the Maharishi, Lisa says: "I remember being kind of surprised by it, but my consciousness wasn't raised enough at that time. I thought it was just the thing (a phase, perhaps) to do at the time. But the Beatles were trailblazers in so many realms. They probably helped open a lot of people's eyes."

She later adds: "Meditation has always been an enigma for me. I'm not very good at it, but I understand Transcendental Meditation now."

Beatles fan Deborah says, "I have tried regular meditation at times in my life, but until recently I have not had a regular meditation practice. I have not tried Transcendental Meditation at all. I researched it a little, but while the idea of repeating a mantra isn't really appealing to me, I can see where it would help to focus the mind."

In terms of when the Beatles fans I interviewed began applying a more spiritual approach to their life, their answers confirmed my theory that for most, it did not happen until after the Beatles wave subsided. For some of them, it opened a career in esoteric studies.

Gordon began reading books about life in his search for meaning, written by authors like Carlos Castenada, Carl Rogers, Carl Jung and others: "I took off after college, traveled out to the West Coast hitch hiking, met a gnostic teacher/master in northern California."

When asked if at any point he embraced spirituality in his choice of career, he replies:

> Interesting question. My teacher gave me a reading at the time and said my mission was to become a cosmic healer. I really had no idea what that meant, but he did say many times healers had to go through their own experiences which sometimes meant suffering, something which I became well familiar with. My work experiences were somewhat linear but never really stable until I got a job at the university as a gardener when I was 39 and worked there until I was 65. It gave me the financial stability that allowed me to pursue my spiritual growth and development to this day. I basically "carried the cross" for humanity where I was subjected to some of the same types of things that the Christ had to do, and learned to maintain the light that came to me when I became illuminated while attending my first conference at Virginia Beach

back in 2003. I had to learn how to keep this light vital and alive. My inner healing work for the collective has grown in reach and heights. Most people are still only beginning to realize for themselves, and I am doing everything humanly possible to help wake up the rest of us.

Nan's journey of incorporating spirituality in her life and in her work began in the early 1980s. When she and her husband Carlos moved to Edinburgh to work on their PhDs, she dropped all organized religion from her life:

I am still working in scientific parapsychology and my interests still surround consciousness and survival research. My day job is teaching graduate level psychology, but now that I am curating my husband's work, and beginning to work on publishing projects that involve his work—which was always more involved with survival research than mine—I am narrowing my interests back to those that, to a great extent, evolved from the spirituality that was reinforced by their journey.

When asked how the Beatles were influential in that coming about, Nan says: "I think it was having permission from people I admired and had incorporated into my understanding of life as a teenager that made a lot of things possible. And that they reinforced a Zeitgeist that re-introduced the Eastern ideas to Western discourse made a huge difference."

Rich was introduced to transcendental meditation while on furlough between Navy electronics schools:

> At that time, I visited with a couple of high school friends who were in college. They were kind enough to show me the ropes at their colleges. One was in a party fraternity and we had some fun with drink and loud music. The other one was more studious, showed me his projects, introduced me to his friends and to transcendental meditation. I was intrigued but not taken enough to seek out that path. The exposure, however, raised my awareness a notch and helped later on.

Nan had a mystical experience that she attributes to the Beatles influence:

> When I was a teenager and meditating, while listening to Ravi Shankar and one of his sitar albums–which I wouldn't have known about if it hadn't been for the Beatles–I had a kind of separation of consciousness that reinforced my belief in reincarnation. Just a fleeting conviction that this person with my name who was meditating

was one of many that I had been in the life of my soul. I was never able to reproduce that feeling, but I still remember it very clearly, and in its immediate aftermath, thought about it a lot.

Afterwards, Nan did some research to learn more about that experience and how to apply it to her life: "While I was already reading all kinds of books about scientific parapsychology and a couple of books about Cayce and reincarnation, I started to buy books about Transcendental Meditation."

Jeannie says that it wasn't until she was on her own that she felt free to do the things she felt were right for her:

> I went to yoga training, took up meditation, and went to Unity. I also studied Reiki, Angels, crystals, Shamanism, the works of Edgar Cayce and became a certified Tarot reader and advisor. In each of these, there is a spiritual foundation and as Swami Satchidananda taught, there are many paths to our One Source. I still work in technology but I have a dedicated room full of crystals, incense, feathers, drums and rattles. I meditate in this space and use my antique singing bowls to open my heart. I find that I now have more clarity of who I am, and the people I let closest to me are those that understand that this is my life.

Like me, Susan had visions of grandeur where the Beatles were concerned. Neither one of us was content to be merely a fan: "More than anything, I wanted to move to London eventually, where I would work for the Beatles and write *the* definitive Beatles biography. That didn't happen, but it was a great dream!"

Also like me, Susan began to immerse herself in metaphysical studies in her early college years: "My college library had an excellent section on mysticism, parapsychology, and metaphysics, so I quickly began devouring everything I could on these topics. After learning more about the concept of reincarnation, so many things began to make sense to me in a way they never did before."

Susan's exposure to spirituality came much earlier when she was an adolescent:

> One of my great aunts was a psychic. I never met her, but I was well acquainted with her daughter, who was also a psychic and attended a spiritualist church in Canton, Ohio. By the time I was a teenager, I had a deep interest in ESP and my best friend and I regularly consulted the Ouija board—often with questions about the Beatles. Its information wasn't very accurate, as we never did meet them, but a door had definitely been opened, one that a few years later after my beliefs had been torn apart and shattered, enabled me to put them back together in a way that truly made

sense and gave me the answers I had been looking for and needed.

Susan did not know anything about Transcendental
Meditation prior to being exposed to it through the Beatles, but she says later when she was in her mid-twenties,
she went to a series of classes/lectures at a small metaphysical bookstore in a nearby town: "It was here that I first
learned about Edgar Cayce and the A.R.E. Meditation, but
not TM, was a part of each of our classes. These classes
were my introduction to and, therefore, first real experiences with meditation."

Deborah is not only a fellow Beatles fan, but also a
fellow graduate of Atlantic University, where I obtained
both my Masters in Transpersonal Studies and my Spiritual
Mentor Certification.

When I started to become more spiritual and
decided to go for a master's degree, the Atlantic
University degree seemed the next logical step, as
it would encompass everything I had been reading and thinking. My culminating project was
"A Transpersonal Approach to Office Politics"
and I learned so much. In my last position as an
Outplacement Counselor, I used those principles with my candidates every day. I had to do it
from a practical position, of course, but imagery,
reframing, positive thinking, self-knowledge, and

self-care were all part of what I used to help the folks I was working with.

Lisa embraced spirituality in her career when she was in her early forties. "I was a 'reluctant messiah,' she says, "and it took me many years to start getting involved in anything, because I didn't want to be influenced by 'group think.' But, as you know, I went on to become a Science of Mind minister, credentialed counselor, and a regressionist. I've been an avid reader, and it has been great confirmation of my beliefs."

Lisa adds that she could not say definitively that the Beatles influenced her decision to follow that path, "with the exception of coming to an understanding of them seeking their own spiritual enlightenment. But their music is a constant comfort and friend in my life, and yes, a spiritual experience as I listen to them."

The Beatles music was the gateway to a spiritual lifestyle for many fans. Certain songs just struck a nerve and sent us on a mystical journey of our own. "They helped set the tone, along with many other song writers and singers," Gordon says. "Many times now I hear a song and am reminded how extraordinary these four were. There had to be a divine purpose for them coming together."

Deborah intuitively knew that the Beatles were going down a more spiritual path when, in her words, "their music became more melodious and richer. I consciously realized it in their psychedelic period. By that time, I was in college and wasn't following them as closely. I was not a fan of the psychedelic music, and I didn't like the idea that they were getting into drugs."While her favorite Beatle was Paul when she was fourteen, as she grew older, she started to follow George's career more closely, saying his albums were the only ones she purchased after the Beatles broke up. Of all of George's music, it was "My Sweet Lord" that she resonated to the most. She admired that George could write a song about God that did not sound like a hymn.

"At that point I still wasn't ready to get back into any religion and I wasn't yet aware that it was really all up to me," Deborah said. "But it was very soon after hearing his new, more spiritual music that I realized that God was in me and not something outside of me to worship only on Sunday. I also started to realize that spirituality is more about how you live your life and not what you do on Sunday or just in front of other people."

Each fan listed his or her favorite song—the one(s) that said something to them. For Susan, one of those songs was "Let it Be." Reflecting on that piece, she says: "More than once, I've read that Paul wrote this song after having a dream in which his mother came and reassured him that things were going to be alright. This aspect alone lends a very spiritual quality to 'Let It Be.' I had a similar experience shortly after the death of an immediate family member."

Deborah and Lisa agreed that "Let It Be" was a spiritually influential piece of music. "It's the message of connecting with spirit and accepting what is," Deborah says.

Joy cited "Imagine" as a song that profoundly affected her. "It is the vision of the world we all want," she says.

It was with great satisfaction that I discovered that the spiritual influence the Beatles had on me was also felt by other Beatle fans. Joy aptly describes how her spiritual life was impacted by the group:

> I would not say the Beatles were gods to me, but they were a huge source of spiritual uplift-ment, joy and hope. Now that we understand how sound vibrations affects us, I think there was something about their music that changed our brain waves. They gave us hope, especially in America where we were suffering from pro-found grief with the assassination of our presi-dent. Their music coincided with the cultural and political revolutions of the 1960s when we were becoming more compassionate, creative, and passionate about justice. These are all spiri-tual qualities, in my opinion. Individually, all four Beatles are examples of using fame and wealth for good, and living their lives as kind human beings. They certainly had—and have—their faults, but so do we all. Nevertheless, their music and their personalities coalesced to profoundly change the world for the better.

Deborah never thought about the connection between her spiritual pursuits and her admiration of the Beatles. "Until this [project], I never would have considered that the Beatles took me on a spiritual ride," she says. "Even though I know that all music speaks to a certain vibrational energy that will sync with our own, until this, I thought the Beatles were just another popular band of my teen years. But the fact that their music has endured is a testament to their connection to spirit and therefore to all of us."

Like the others who participated in answering questions about how the Beatles influenced their spirituality, Rich never thought about crediting the Beatles for his spiritual awakening: "But as my life has unfolded, I realize that there was, at least, the influence that was on-going as I would listen and re-listen to their music and study the lyrics." He adds:

> It was certainly a reinforcing aspect from time to time when I would get distracted and slip off my path into the gutter. Listening to them would often help me climb back up onto the path and even shed much needed light. Over the years, these songs grew in their meaning and influence on my path as it wound along. They often changed color as my perception needed a different perspective at various times. Frankly, the A.R.E. and Edgar Cayce's principles on life and all that that brought to my awareness was the

turning point for me. It was quite the transformation in my life. Since that world opened to me in 1972, I have enjoyed a bright light on my path, showing the way to spiritualization of my physical experience in this lifetime.

Lisa states that her spiritual journey may have been influenced by the Beatles before she was even aware of it. "Music, in itself, is a spiritual journey for me," she says. "Their music is always like coming home, being surrounded in a huge embrace of familiar territory, bringing me peace, comfort, and many memories. Melodies are crucial for me and settle me into a space that allows me to be more open. 'The Long and Winding Road' is one such melody."

Julie put more thought into how her spiritual journey was impacted by the Beatles: "The Beatles were the catalyst that sparked my interest and exploration." She adds:

I don't believe in coincidence. I believe that, as a willing traveler, I embarked on a journey to discover some of what life could hold in store for the curious, to discern what fit in my framework of values, and to adopt what made most sense given a zillion variables ... I think my spiritual exploration, initiated by the Beatles, opened my willingness to an unimaginable suite of cultural and religious experiences (including ultimately circling back to Catholicism) that would otherwise have been unrecognized as unique opportunities. The Beatles gave me just the right nudge at the right time to get started. Yeah, yeah, yeah.

Lisa says that her whole life has been influenced by the Beatles:

They are heroes to me of their time and their talent and their ability to just be themselves through it all. I measure all music up to theirs, and while I have other musicians that I love, nothing reaches the level of love that has encompassed my life because of them. They are home. They are family. They are cherished. I am always full of gratitude for being alive at the same time they were at the peak of their popularity and influence. I'm not a spiritual being because of them, but I recognize their genius in being transparent about their path, which allows me to be open and transparent about mine. I have often wished I could have had a conversation with John or George and gotten into their heads a bit about their beliefs. Isn't it interesting that they are the two who were gone so soon? But George knew where he was going.

And now, so do we.

Chapter Eight

Soul Writers

There are several key components of my spiritual career that I shared with the Beatles, but did not realize the extent of that connection until recently. My professional pursuit of reincarnation research and therapy was done in conjunction with studying another spiritual phenomenon—one I later named Soul Writing™. Referred to as "Inspirational Writing" by Edgar Cayce, and wrongly labeled "Automatic Writing" by those who don't know better, Soul Writing is best described as a written form of meditation. If you think of prayer as you talking to God, and meditation as God talking to you, Soul Writing is you taking notes. It is writing in an altered state of consciousness and it is a process that has been used for centuries by famous writers, composers, and artists.

In my first book, *Soul Writing: Conversing With Your Higher Self*, I explore what it's like to write in an altered state of consciousness and all the ways it can be applied to your life, including using it to enhance your psychic abilities; in past-life exploration; obtaining guidance on specific topics; in various art forms; delving deeper into esoteric philosophies; in psychoanalysis and healing; writing for soul's growth; and in service to others.

In researching others who employed Soul Writing into their work, I learned of many famous writers who struggled to describe the process of inspiration. They knew they were being divinely influenced, but did not fully comprehend the source of that inspiration. Musical composers obtain their inspiration the same way that literary writers do, recording that inspiration as musical notes rather than the written word. For instance, John's method of writing the lyrics to "Across the Universe" is an example of how this type of guided writing manifests itself.

According to Steve Turner, John claimed the lyrics came to him while he was in bed at Kenwood. ". . . as he lay there trying to sleep, the phrase 'pools of sorrow, waves of joy' came to him and wouldn't leave until he got up and started writing the words down," Turner writes. He quotes John as saying: "It drove me out of bed. I didn't want to write it. I was just slightly irritable and I couldn't go to sleep."

That same process revealed itself earlier when John wrote "Nowhere Man." John claimed the song came from his subconscious. After spending hours trying to write something meaningful, he took a break. As he was resting, the words and music came to him, seemingly out of nowhere, and he felt compelled to write them down. This is as good a definition of Soul Writing as I can find.

John's description of how the lyrics came to him for "Across the Universe" and "Nowhere Man" had similarities to the process described by great writers and composers alike. I believe all people are creative in one form or another, but I wonder whether people like John are able to tap into a deeper well than others. My research discovered that many artists, composers, and writers have learned—whether by accident or intentionally—to access an unseen dimension that for them becomes an endless fountain from which their creative genius flows. They reach that invisible world by entering an altered state of consciousness brought about by trance, meditation, or dreams. While in this altered state, the quality of their work reaches new heights, vastly different in style, tone and composition than work done in their waking state. This is certainly what happened with John as the words "came to him" while he was in a quiet space. He was in good company. The English poet Percy Shelley writes: "One after another the greatest writers, poets, and artists confirm the fact that their work comes to them from beyond the threshold of consciousness." That phrase—beyond the threshold of consciousness—is an apt description of meditation.

Rudyard Kipling admitted that the key to gaining access to his inner helper was "not to think consciously, but to drift," also another way of describing meditation. Author Richard Bach had an experience that mirrored John's. He was walking one day when he heard an inner voice repeat: "Jonathan Livingston Seagull." He went home and began writing furiously, trying to keep up with the flow of words that were coming spontaneously to mind.

You may be surprised at how this inspirational process worked for famous composers as well. In describing his creative process, Wolfgang Amadeus Mozart writes: "Whence and how they come, I know not; nor can I force them."

Beethoven says a "canon" came into his head while he napped during a carriage ride. When he awoke, he remembered it and committed it to paper.

Johannes Brahms told a biographer that the inspiration for his most famous compositions came to him from ideas that flowed through him from God. He admitted that he had to be "in a semi-trance condition to get such results—a condition when the conscious mind is in temporary abeyance, and the subconscious mind is in control." Sound familiar?

Russian composer Tchaikovsky describes a similar process—an urgent sense of needing to write something down quickly: "I forget everything and behave like a mad man; everything within me starts pulsing and quivering; hardly have I begun the sketch, ere one thought follows another."

Composer Richard Strauss describes how music flowed through him: "It seemed to me that I was dictated to by two wholly different Omnipotent Entities . . . I was definitely conscious of being aided by more than an earthly Power, and it was responsive to my determined suggestions."

Meditation is one of several key components necessary for soul writing. No one understood better the connection between meditation and creativity than George Harrison. In an interview with his former sister-in-law, Dr. Jenny Boyd, George drew the correlation between the two. "Meditation is only a means to an end," he said. "In order to infuse energy and power and get it flowing through our bodies, we have to meditate. You infuse that energy into your being, and so when you are in activity, it rubs off onto that creatively. To really be in touch with creative energy, you will find that it lies within the stillness."

The time John and Paul spent with the Maharishi enabled them to learn the benefits of meditation and apply it toward their songwriting. In *The Lyrics*, Paul acknowledges the benefits of meditation, saying: "It's very hard to just be still and let a mantra simply roll around in your head . . . My mind is so active that it's good to attempt to shut out all those little things that get in your way, trying to trip you up."

George also commented on the need for quieting his mind when composing, telling Dr. Jenny Boyd: "I like quietness. I tend to write most of my songs in the night when the world goes to sleep for a bit and everything's quiet."

Paul understood that meditation was a powerful tool where songwriting was concerned. Talking about his method of writing a song, he said it isn't so much that he composes them, but rather they arrive. Meditation helps that process and often creates an opening for a song.

In discussing what could arguably be described as his greatest composition, *Yesterday,* Paul says: "The great thing about *Yesterday* is that it kind of wrote itself. People say to me, 'Do you believe in mysticism or magic?' With that story, I kind of have to . . . I just *dreamed* it, what a gift." Meyers wrote that this factor concerned Paul so much that he worried he'd be accused of plagiarism as he didn't feel that song was his. This is a common retort among those experimenting with Soul Writing. The words that come to them are much deeper and more profound than anything they have ever written in a conscious state, leaving them to question their origin. But if John and Paul don't own it, who does?

John says something similar regarding "Across the Universe." He said the words were purely inspirational and were given to him. As such, he couldn't claim ownership. For John, writing as if he were possessed was a joy in that he was acting as a medium between himself and whoever or whatever was supplying the inspiration.

One of the most common questions I hear by those engaged in Soul Writing, is who is doing the writing? Is it their spirit guide? An angel? An ascended master? Source itself? Or perhaps a Muse? Meyers explores the idea of the Muse at work in the Beatles music, citing John's mother Julia as his Muse; Paul's mother Mary as his Muse:

> The muse phenomenon is mysterious and fas-
> cinating, tantalizing us to consider some form
> of relationship with another realm. What exactly
> is a muse? An angel or spirit guide, some type

of ghost or disembodied being? Could it be the consciousness, soul or spirit of a dead person? The muse is thought to inspire, but what is inspiration? The word breaks down to "in," "spirit" and the suffix "tion" involves action. To put it together, the word means "embodying spirit in action." Inspiration can involve receptivity to a muse, a way to channel the divine. These "beings," or however we wish to construe them, play this mediating role, the bridging of worlds. The muse is the deliverer of "heaven" into the realm of earth.

Meyers quotes author Stephen King who, when asked how he comes up with the ideas for his books, says: "Good story ideas seem to come quite literally from nowhere, sailing at you right out from the empty sky . . . Your job isn't to find these ideas, but to recognize them when they show up."

According to Meyers, John and Paul have "uttered statements about their songwriting process consistent with this notion. The work is to attune consciousness to the creative void of this nowhere land. It could occur in meditation and some report enhanced receptivity in altered states. The main way these songwriters receive their inspiration, how they connect with their muse, appears to be through dreaming." Meyers later explains that for the Beatles:

The muse process was mainly unconscious, especially early on. However, the astrology for the inspired songs provides a map through the fogginess. Her role is detected, understood and given a broader context. Other facets of the songs, including ways to decipher messages or teachings, are revealed. Existing in another dimension or plane of consciousness, the muse could have access to broader archetypal, symbolic or mythological realms. Her role is to bring such heavenly perspectives to illuminate our experience on Earth.

John's song, "Nowhere Man," came about the same way. The song parallels the process Paul went through with "Yesterday." Ian MacDonald, British music critic and author of *Revolution in the Head: The Beatles' Records and the Sixties*, claims both songs arrived in a "quasi-mediumistic way. "Nowhere Man," he says, is "'equally untypical of Lennon' as "Yesterday" was for McCartney, supporting the idea of discovery rather than creation."

Meyers later states, "John was aware he was receiving a vision, the message and music arrived as he 'lay down.' Connection with the muse informs the songwriting, but also assists the healing of John's underlying issue of death and loss."

"He [John] says the song 'came through,' but from whom and how?" asks Meyers. "Other songs are speculated to be inspired, meaning what John and Paul were writing may be their own personalized version of such inspiration . . . 'Across the Universe' may be the clearest example of actual words coming directly from the muse."

I tell students of Soul Writing that they are the ones doing the writing. It is coming from a divine source, through their soul, and then out on paper. They did the writing themselves, with a little help from their friends.

As with Soul Writing, the intended outcome is to elicit some form of healing. According to Meyers, that is exactly what "Across the Universe" does. Writing about the composition, Meyers says: "The result of such mystical transmission is healing. The song continues with the Sanskrit line, 'Jai Guru Deva Om.' One interpretation is 'glory to the shining remover of darkness,' a sentiment consistent with spiritual awakening."

Paul's composition of "Let It Be" came about through much the same process. Meyers writes that Paul is "consistently clear that the experience felt like a visitation, a non-ordinary experience, rather than a thought or memory." Meyers says the theme of 'Let It Be' is that Spirit is always with us and that Spiritual light is eternal. He acknowledges that Paul "crafted a timeless song that is healing, transformative and inspired. 'Let It Be' invites us all to emotionally connect, to heal our initial spiritual amnesia, to reunite with eternal light."

Those are the very concepts explored in great depth through the Soul Writing process—a process that Paul,

John and George utilized in their song writing without really understanding what it was or where it originated.

If you're curious about how to do Soul Writing, you can read my book *Soul Writing: Conversing With Your Higher Self*; schedule a private Soul Writing session with me via my website (www.joannedimaggio.com); or read through the step-by-step instructions provided at the end of the book.

Chapter Nine

Get Back: The Beatles on Reincarnation and Other Metaphysical Concepts

Thinking about the years I spent heading up the fan club, I can see how effortlessly the Beatles transitioned from the mop tops we all adored to the gurus who provided spiritual lessons that gradually awakened us to a new level of understanding life. This may have been why, as we grew older, we lost patience with our younger counterparts. We were slowly getting the message, but were they?

The Beatles were aware of the challenge of connecting to their audience. According to Eric Meyers:

The growth and change the last couple of years was rapid and profound, they had completely moved beyond the adolescent consciousness of the early formula and its massive popularity. Songs like 'Tomorrow Never Knows' or 'Within You Without You' flew over many peoples' heads.

Messages which contain another dimension or perspective can bring confusion or discomfort and are easily distorted. Those who are not on the same wavelength often dismiss or sometimes ridicule what is not understood.

As mentioned earlier, my world shifted when I first heard "Tomorrow Never Knows." If I were hard pressed to select a favorite Beatles song, even now, that would be it. The phrases resonated with me on a deep, previously unexplored part of my psyche. To this day, when I play that song, I turn up the volume, close my eyes, relax and "float downstream."

It wasn't until I read Eric Meyers's book, that I learned that John wanted to mimic the sound coming from the Dalai Lama and Tibetan monks chanting on a mountaintop. I did know, however, that the song was influenced by *The Tibetan Book of the Dead*. The song may have been associated with LSD, as Meyers says, but it had nothing to do with drugs where I was concerned. Instead, the lyrics and the music felt as though they were a slow moving one-passenger boat heading downstream to some mystical destination. As Meyers explains it: "The motion is from the level of thought (mind) to pure being (soul), bringing us to the Transcendence phase. Floating downstream relates to the stream of consciousness, the dreaming process. With a relaxed mind, consciousness can 'surrender to the void,' which is being described as 'shining.' Dreaming is brought to the context of soul awareness, our connection with the eternal spiritual life force."

As I mentioned earlier, my favorite phrase in "Tomorrow Never Knows," is "play the game existence to the end . . . of the beginning." What better way to describe reincarnation?

Another reference to reincarnation came in George's "I Want to Tell You," when he says, "I could wait forever, I've got time," and later, "maybe next time around." He brings up reincarnation again in "It's All Too Much" when he sings: "Floating down the stream of time, of life to life with me."

While I eventually looked at the Beatles as a source of many spiritual lessons, it seemed to me that as far as conveying deeply-rooted spiritual truths, George was light years beyond the others. He was a most remarkable, wise teacher—the kind who would command a packed classroom because you did not want to miss a single word he had to say. Not everyone got the message, even though it was all there, right in front of our eyes. You had to connect your ears with your mind and your soul before any changes happened.

I felt the shift happening when John repeated, "Can you hear me?" in "Rain," and I could honestly say, "Yes, John. I hear you!" This shift in consciousness ultimately ended my Beatles Fan Club days. It put me into some sort of mystical cocoon, only to emerge when *Out on a Limb* was televised.

When I decided in 1987 to focus my career in the area of reincarnation research and studies, I had no idea of the sheer volume of quotes from the Beatles that referenced past lives. As deeply absorbed in their lives as I was, I surely must have read or heard some of the quotes I discovered when I did the research for this book. Yet I don't think in my wildest dreams I would have thought I'd fill page upon page of metaphysical-related quotes attributed to them.

In my spiritual studies over the years, many of the topics commented on by one of the Beatles at an earlier point in time, echoed what I discovered in the books, classes and conferences I attended. This was especially true as I got into a deeper study of the Edgar Cayce readings. Now the very philosophies that I teach and incorporate in writing my books can be found in quotes from one of the Beatles. I do believe that you can hear something quite clearly at one point in time, file it away somewhere in your sub-conscious mind, only to have it surface when the time is right. In my case, their words of wisdom and profound understanding of how the universe operated, came back to support my own theories.

I'd like to explore the pertinent quotes from the Beatles that coincide with my spiritual studies, especially on the topic of reincarnation. Many of these quotes came about as a reflection of the aftermath of John's comments about being more popular than Jesus. Tobias Churton put it this way: "The 'we're more popular than Jesus' controversy . . . signaled a period when the group would find its identity inseparable from spiritual issues, and what would soon appear to be a new, and for many threatening, spiritual landscape."

Threatening indeed. It wasn't so much that John said the group was more popular than Jesus, but that he also likened each of us to being God. Churton quoted a comment John made to the *Daily Express* journalist David Wigg:

> Wigg asked about an interview where the pop star seemed to have said that he was God. *Did he believe that he was God?* "Not *the* God, not *the* God," corrected Lennon. "But we're all God, and we're all potentially divine, and potentially evil. We have everything within us. And it's no good blaming God for war because you can use the H-power, the atomic power, whatever it is, to light a room, or you can kill people with it with a bomb."

Good Lord—can you imagine the reaction of any religious sect to that comment? It's important to understand the Beatles and their relationship to God, Source, Creator—whatever they considered their higher power. In a reference from *In Their Own Words: The Beatles . . . after the Break-Up,* John is quoted as saying: "I believe that God is like a power-house, like where you keep electricity, like a power station. And He's the supreme power, and that He's neither good nor bad, left, right, black or white. He just is.

And we tap that source of power and make it what we will. Just as electricity can kill people in a chair, or you can light a room with it. I think God is."

Barry Miles, writing in *Beatles In Their Own Words*, quoted a rare statement from Paul about his belief in God. "God is in everything. God is in the space between us. God is in the table in front of you. It just happens I realise all this through acid. It could have been through anything else."

In that same book, Miles quotes George as saying:

We've all got the same goal whether we realise it or not. We're all striving for something which is called God. For a reunion, complete. Everybody has realized at some time or other that no matter how happy they are, there's still always the unhappiness that comes with it . . . Everyone is a potential Jesus Christ, really. We are all trying to get to where Jesus Christ got. And we're going to be on this world until we get there. We're all different people and we are all doing different things in life, but that doesn't matter because the whole point of life is to harmonize with everything, every aspect in creation . . . Everybody is potentially divine. It's just a matter of self-realisation before it will all happen . . . The Beatles got all the material wealth that we needed and that was enough to show us that this thing wasn't material. We are all in the physical world, yet what we are striving for isn't physical. We all get so hung up with material things like cars and televisions and houses, yet what they can give you is only there for a little bit and then it's gone . . . I'm a musician. I don't know why. This is a thing that I've looked back on since my birth.

George goes on to comment on one of the foundational tenets of reincarnation—the overriding element of free will and how at any given time we can change the course of our lives—and our karma—simply by the choices we make:

Many people feel that life is pre-destined. I think it is vaguely, but it's still up to you which way your life's going to go. All I've ever done is to keep being me and it's just all worked out. It just did it all . . . magic . . . it just did it. We never planned anything. So it's obvious—because I'm a musician now, that's what I was destined to be. It's my gig.

George comments further on his fate at becoming a Beatle, karma and free will:

Although we do have control over our actions right at this moment, I think what we are now is a result of our past actions, and what we're going to be is going to be a result of our present actions. So for certain things there's no way out. There's no way I wasn't going to be in The Beatles, even though I didn't know. In retrospect that's what it was, it was a set-up. At the same time, I do have control over my actions. I can do good actions or bad actions. Like I say, I can try being a pop star forever and go on TV and do concerts and be a celebrity. Or I can be a gardener.

Many people wonder if life is pre-destined. If it is, who draws up the contract on what issues we will face in the next life? Can this contract be renegotiated? What role does free will have to play in determining a change of direction? Over the years, I had many clients who blamed their problems on everyone except themselves. Yet I knew from my years of reincarnation studies that each of us is responsible for designing the life we are living. In 2019, I decided to create a research project to test that theory. Through hypnotic regression, volunteers shared what they experienced in the afterlife, with a specific emphasis on the soul's role in planning the next life. My intent was to challenge, confirm and build on prior research in this field. I was hoping that those who participated in the research would see that the decisions they made prior to coming into this life set up the issues they were dealing with today.

I was especially interested in determining whether there was a common afterlife experience among those who volunteered for the project. My theory was, if all, or at least the majority of participants, remembered their deaths and time spent between lives in much the same way, and if that experience was pleasant, that would dissipate the fear of death. The fact that no one in the project knew each other added to the credibility of the research, as I felt it was all the more believable when they had similar experiences when they entered that place between this life and all the lives prior to this one. Then I hoped they would reexamine their life's experiences as what they are—a path for their soul's growth.

Edgar Cayce referred to death as "God's Other Door." The twenty-five men and women in my research study confirmed his assessment that death was walking through a portal. Without exception, they described death as a gentle, painless, and positive experience giving them a sense of relief and freedom.

So what did the Beatles think about death? Writing in his book, *In Their Own Words: The Beatles . . . After the Breakup,* David Bennahum includes two quotes on that very subject. The first surprised me, as it was attributed to Ringo in a 1980 interview in which he says: "I won't go to funerals because I don't believe in them. I totally believe your soul has gone by the time you get into the limo. She or he's up there or wherever it is. I'm sure . . . I can't wait to go half the time."

In that same book, Bennahum quotes George from a November 1987 interview—the same year I began my spiritual quest. George is reported to have said: "At the bottom line, I think that even if the whole planet blew up, you'd have to think about what happens when you die. In the end, 'Life goes on within you and without you.' I just have a belief that this is only one little bit, the physical world is one little bit, of the physical universe, and you can't really destroy it totally. You can destroy our planet, but the souls are going onto other planets. So in the end it doesn't really matter."

The Beatles were no strangers to death and certainly those personal encounters gave them food for thought about the afterlife. Ironically, George and John were most quoted about their beliefs about life after death, and those were the two we lost first. Still, you only have to look at their comments on the death of family members and close friends to know they gave some thought about what happens when the body dies. Churton writes:

> John Lennon's own religious outlook at the time was somewhat confused . . . Lennon found . . . an attraction for Buddhism because it seemed, at least to begin with, a more scientific approach to enlightenment. That is, if you did certain things, certain "spiritual" results would ensure, chief of which—and the most desirable to John Lennon at the time—being peace of mind, which had been severely disturbed not only by the tempests of Beatlemania but also by the sudden death of

his mother in 1958 and of his close friend Stuart
Sutcliff in Hamburg in 1962.

One aspect of death that is often questioned concerns
the ramifications of suicide. Most metaphysical teachings say that individuals who commit suicide will find
themselves incarnated again, almost immediately. It's the
equivalent of dropping out of school. You didn't finish the
course(s) you signed up for, so you can't move on until
they are complete. Worse yet, the lessons intended to be
learned in the previous life will be that much harder if they
are repeated after a suicide prevented them from being
completed the first time around.

In *Nowhere Man: The final days of John Lennon*, author
Robert Rosen writes that suicide was out of the question
for John for much the same reason: ". . . he believed deeply
in the existence of God. If he killed himself, there'd be a
terrible karmic price to pay."

John also was an avid student of numerology, and
while, as Rosen writes, "there was a lot of good in the
numbers" as far as John's fate was concerned, "The problem was that the bad seemed to overwhelm it; the numbers
were stacked against him. There were too many indications
of catastrophe, violence, premature death. But John didn't
need the *Book of Numbers* to tell him that. He had felt it in
his soul for as long as he could remember. Psychics could
sense it when they looked at him. The numbers only confirmed it."

According to Rosen, John and Yoko had a full-time psychic and tarot card reader, Charlie Swan. One of the reasons Rosen believes John trusted "the O" (for Oracle) was because he never said anything to frighten John: "Even during tarot readings, when the death card itself came up under the most inauspicious circumstances, the O was always able to convince Lennon that it meant rebirth or change, not imminent death. Still, John sensed from the look in the O's eyes that something ominous was hanging over him like a black cloud. John couldn't hide his dark vibrations, and it didn't take a psychic to feel them."

Rosen said John's song, "Borrowed Time," "was a prophetic, haunting statement set to a reggae beat. He simply acknowledges the doom he's felt in his soul for decades. Death may be close by, he says, but that's okay. Death is release. Life is a burden. He's done it all and there's nothing left to do."

Rosen went on to say that there were times, when John was sitting in the morning room looking out at Central Park, that his thoughts turned to the afterlife: "More and more frequently he caught himself daydreaming of the eternal bliss that lay beyond," Rosen wrote. "Yet he certainly did not want to die. Too many things were going well ..."

As most people know, John was murdered on December 8, 1980. George gave much thought to what John was experiencing in the afterlife, but it took him weeks before he would be able to talk about it: "We saw beyond each other's physical bodies," he said, seeking to reassure fans that John's soul lived on. "If you can't feel the spirit of some friend who's been that close, then what chance have you got to feel the spirit of Christ or Buddha or whatever you may be interested in?"

On the popular British talk show, *Aspel & Company,* George adds, "I believe what it says in the scriptures and the Bhagavad Gita: 'Never was there a time when you did not exist, and there will never be a time when you cease to exist.' The only thing that changes is our bodily condition . . . I feel him around here."

Geoffrey Giuliano, author of *Dark Horse: The Private Life of George Harrison,* writes about George's reaction at the death of his mother:

> George was at his mother's bedside when she passed away. Naturally he was deeply troubled and upset by her death, but this was his Krishna conscious period and the teachings of Srila Prabhupada were of great comfort. Thumbing through his already well-worn copy of the guru's *Bhagavad Gita, As It Is,* he silently read and reread everything Sri Krishna had to say about the nature of death in this world. Two verses in particular stood out in his mind. Over the next few years, he would be forced to seek the shelter of their wisdom on several other such occasions:

For the soul there is never birth or death. Nor, having once been, does he ever cease to be. He is unborn, eternal, ever-existing, undying, and primeval. He is not slain when the body is slain.

As a person puts on new garments, giving up old ones; similarly, the soul accepts new material bodies, giving up the old and useless ones.

The death of the Beatles manager, Brian Epstein, had a major impact on the group that ultimately changed the trajectory of their lives. Pattie Boyd, writing in her memoir, *Wonderful Tonight: George Harrison, Eric Clapton, and Me*, remembered George's reaction to Brian's death:

Already George was full of Maharishi's teachings: 'There is no such thing as death,' he said to reporters that Sunday morning in Bangor, 'only in the physical sense. We know he's okay now. He will return because he was striving for happiness and desired bliss so much.' And a little later, he said much the same thing: 'There's no such thing as death anyway. I mean, it's death on a physical level, but life goes on everywhere.' George found it comforting to believe that Brian's soul would be back one day—and I agreed with him.

George acknowledged that life went on after death and he had a unique way of expressing that notion through examples in nature. Tillery quotes George as saying: "The atoms in any object—a plant, for example—do not cease to exist when it dies or is thrown on a trash heap. In time the atoms in any object dissociate, disperse, and are reconfigured in some new form."[1]

There aren't many notations of how Paul felt about death, but I did run across one in *The Beatles, God & The Bible* by Ray Comfort. Speaking about death, Paul is quoted as saying: "When your number's up, it's up ... It's something I don't really think about too much. I'm too busy living."

In that same book, however, Comfort writes that Linda's death seemed to deepen Paul's spirituality. "When CNN's Larry King asked Paul, 'Do you think Linda is somewhere?' he answered, 'Yes, she's here. Sort of. In a kind of dimensional thing. I don't know. I don't—I don't have any sort of very strong religious beliefs. But I have kind of—I have spiritual feelings about that kind of thing.'"

Paul is quoted as saying: "I'm not religious, but I'm very spiritual." Later, in light of the deaths of John and George, Comfort says that Paul began to talk more about "'the Man upstairs,' saying that it was God who would determine when his number was up. The interview revealed that he not only believed in God, but that he also believed in some sort of afterlife."

Geoffrey Giuliano writes: "Denny Laine insists that Paul, especially, is quite the closet mystic, voraciously plowing through book after book on reincarnation, pyramids, karma and the like." Giuliano quotes Laine as saying: "I was frankly a little bit surprised that Paul was into it as much as he was . . . I saw a different side to him; he'd shown me the depths he was capable of."

Unlike John, who had no idea in advance that death would be waiting for him at his doorstep, George knew that he was losing his battle with cancer and that his time was coming to an end. Joshua Greene writes: "From the beginning of his spiritual journey, George knew that his frame of mind at death would determine where his soul would be reborn. 'Whatever state of being one remembers when quitting the body,' he read in the Bhagavad Gita, 'that state one will attain without fail,' and from that time on, he was rarely without the holy names of God on his lips."

Greene also quotes George as saying: "With many lives our association with the temporary has grown. This impermanent body, a bag of bones and flesh, is mistaken for our true self, and we have accepted this temporary condition to be final."

George's thoughts on his impending death were included in *George Harrison: Behind the Locked Door*. "There was no major shift in perspective," Graeme Thompson writes. "The illusion of physical death, after all, was a subject he had been contemplating since his early twenties. 'The soul keeps on going,' he said. 'I know that to be true. It's not something I just made up to make myself feel good.'"

In *I Me Mine,* George Harrison, talks more about dying: "Everybody is worried about dying, but the cause of death (which most can't figure out unless they are diseased) is birth, so if you don't want to die you don't get born! So, the 'art of dying' is when somebody can consciously leave the body at death, as opposed to falling down dying without knowing what's going on. The Yogi who does that (Maha-samadhi) doesn't have to reincarnate again."

His lyrics in "The Art of Dying" express a matter-of-fact attitude George had toward death. The first verse is about death and its inevitability:

> *There will come a time when all of us must leave here*
> *Then nothing sister Mary can do*
> *Will keep me here with you.*

The last verse is about reincarnation:

> *There will come a time when most of us return here*
> *Brought back by our desire to be a perfect entity.*

George put it this way:

Well our soul's desire is perfect. The last thought or desire that we have as we are leaving our physical bodies, that (thought or desire) is the motivation for rebirth. It's all right going through your life forgetting about God and then, as you are dying, hoping to be able to remember Him then, or remember something that is liberating. You are leaving your body—which could be at any moment. I mean I don't want to be lying there as I'm dying thinking, 'Oh shit, I forgot to put the cat out,' or, 'I didn't get a Rolls-Royce,' because then you may have to come right back just to do those things, and then you have got more knots on your piece of string.

"Death," according to George in The Beatles *SOLO*, "is just where your suit falls off and now you're in your other suit. It's all right. Don't worry."

There are many aspects of metaphysical topics that one can specialize in. I've already mentioned how I've come to lean in the direction of reincarnation studies. Certainly comments made by George constituted a treasure-trove of affirmations about the reality of reincarnation.

One of my favorite analogies in explaining reincarnation is to see Earth as a school. Before we come into a body and are still in the afterlife between lives, we review our past lives with the Elders, a group of wise beings who are akin to our guidance counselors in school. They review our lives like counselors would review a report card, and based on the lessons we've passed, we need to repeat, or haven't taken yet, they help us design the next life. Together, we create the class curriculum we will take on in the next life, as well as the karmic attributes we will bring with us to help us with those lessons.

Meyers references that analogy: "We can think of Earth like a school where we learn how to grow and consciously reconnect with healing spiritual nourishment."

George uses the analogy of going to school as well: "Each person has to find for himself a way for inner realization. I still believe that's the only reason we're on this planet. It's like going to school again: each soul is potentially divine and the goal is to manifest that divinity. Everything else is secondary."

Another analogy I use in teaching reincarnation, is that we are spiritual beings having an experience in a human body. I often compare the body to a vehicle. It's all shiny and new when we first inhabit it, but then over the years it needs repair and eventually it's time to trade it in for another vehicle. George refers to his incarnation much the same way, with these lyrics from "Living in the Material World":

I got born into the material world
Getting worn out in the material world
Use my body like a car
Taking me both near and far
Met my friends all in the material world

Tillery adds: "In his own mystical view, he was a bit of Krishna temporarily inhabiting a body known as George

Harrison. To achieve release from the endless round of reincarnation, it is essential not to become too attached."[2]

George knew enough about reincarnation to understand that his deep interest in the religions of India had to do with his own past-life journey. Ray Comfort quotes George as addressing this: "I got to understand what Christ really was through Hinduism. Down through the ages there has always been the spiritual path, it's been passed on, it always will be, and if anybody ever wants it in any age it's always there . . . It may be something to do with my past lives, but I felt a great connection with it."

John Blake, writing in *All You Needed Was Love: The Beatles After the Beatles,* summed it up this way: "George's first desperate passion for India and her myriad philosophies had later matured into a quieter love, and he had begun to live his life loosely according to Hindu principles, with an unshakable belief in the law of *karma*—the doctrine of the inevitable consequences of every act we commit—which made his greatest pleasure giving his money away to anyone who came to him with a plausible request."

Although George never made it to 90, and I'm certainly not there yet, I cannot help but smile when I read this insightful quote: "Now I understand about 90-year-old people who feel like teenagers because nothing changes. It's just the body that changes. The soul in the body is there at birth and there at death. The only change is the bodily condition."

The theme of reincarnation is prevalent in the lyrics of many of George's other songs. For instance, in *Circles*, he writes:

Soul takes on a body with each birth we make our date
With life and death along the road the soul reincarnates
The show goes round and round in circles

In the course of my research, it was nearly impossible to find a quote from Ringo Starr concerning his spiritual beliefs. I did find one attributed to him that was shared by George. "Ringo wants to know if he could come back as a cat. 'I like cats' he told me and laughed."

For the record, while there are some cultures who believe souls move in and out of both human and animal bodies, my studies are clear. Humans don't come back as animals, and the souls of animals don't migrate into human bodies. That's a topic for an entirely different book!

John and Yoko also delved into the theory of reincarnation. Ray Comfort writes: "John and Yoko participated in seances . . . Yoko also collected Egyptian things because she thought they had magical powers, and John wanted to find the spear used to pierce Jesus' side because he was certain that with it, he could do anything in the universe."

Robert Rosen, in describing Yoko's office, wrote that those "Egyptian things" she collected were actually 26th Dynasty Egyptian antiques that were acquired during their January 1979 trip to the pyramids outside Cairo:

"John had accompanied Yoko on this field trip and they had spent a night inside The Great Pyramid, an experience that thrilled and energized the Lennons, heightening their magical powers—or so Yoko said."

Even more interesting, according to Rosen, John and Yoko believed that they were the reincarnation of Victorian poets Robert Browning and Elizabeth Barrett Browning. Rosen said on the last page of John's diary, he copied a verse from a work of Browning: "John was so enchanted by Browning's lines that he used them in his own song, recorded during the *Double Fantasy* sessions but included instead on *Milk and Honey*. The lines were: *Grow old along with me! The best is yet to be.*"

In terms of John and Paul's belief in reincarnation, Gary Tillery writes:

Lennon reserved judgment about the possibility that the individual personality or spirit could survive physical death. Paul McCartney acknowledged that the Beatles had discussed life after death and all four had pledged that the one who died first would try to communicate with the others. Lennon also promised his son Julian that if anything happened to him, he would send a sign to verify he was all right—a feather would appear to him in a closed room and drift down to the floor.[3]

A white feather was eventually gifted to Julian and it was a very profound moment for him. Julian tells it this way:

> One thing Dad said to me should he pass away, if there was any way of letting me know he was going to be ok the message would come to me in the form of a white feather. Then something happened to me about ten years ago when I was on tour in Australia. I was presented with a white feather by an Aboriginal tribal elder, which definitely took my breath away. One thing for sure is that the white feather always represented peace to me.

In 2007, Julian founded The White Feather Foundation, whose mission is to "embrace environmental and humanitarian issues; and in conjunction with partners from around the world, help to raise funds for the betterment of all life."

There are many ways to uncover past lives. I don't know whether John, Paul, George or Ringo used meditation as a key to unlock the door to their own past lives, whether intentionally or by accident. Entering into an altered state of consciousness, listening to that still small voice within, allowing the subconscious to come forward to share the past-life memories stored in the soul, is something obtained through meditation, and we know all four engaged in a meditation practice at some point.

Music can produce a similar result. Certain music, with its peculiar vibrations, can activate past-life memories. Joshua Greene writes: "Talking about the lyrics on his album, *Chants of India*, in an interview from VH-1, he [George] said: ". . . listen to something that has its roots in transcendence. The words of these songs carry a very subtle spiritual vibration that goes beyond the intellect, really. If you let yourself be free . . . it can have a very positive effect."

About John's experience with meditation, Tillery writes that despite John's less than stellar opinion of the Maharishi, Lennon benefited from the instruction he received on how to meditate. "For the rest of his life, he often turned to meditation to restore himself and improve his creativity. He characterized his use of it as 'mysticism,' but not in a supernatural or religious sense."[4]

"Lennon found it therapeutic to still the conscious mind and slip out of day-to-day preoccupations,"[5] Tillery adds.

Rosen agrees: "[Meditation] cleared his mind, relaxed him. Outside of walking, yoga was the only exercise he ever did. But spiritual rather than physical reasons motivated him to continue meditating."

Rosen said John's greatest ambition was to achieve a state of spiritual perfection: "John believed that if he meditated long and hard enough, he'd merge with God and acquire psychic powers, like clairvoyance and the ability to fly through the air. And he wanted those powers as badly as he wanted anything. Yoko wanted him to have them, and she urged him to keep meditating."

Visualization is another method to access past-life memories, and I often use guided imagery as a method to quiet the conscious mind and focus on the images coming from another time and another place.

John also used visualization as inspiration for writing his music, a technique Yoko had introduced him to years earlier. Tillery writes: "The technique has an occult derivation, the idea being that on some ethereal level we are constantly in contact with the forces of the universe and that our heartfelt wishes, our prayers, communicate through the cosmos and can attract to us what we desire."[6]

John and Yoko were partners in every sense of the word, especially when pursuing spiritual guidance. As stated earlier, in addition to astrology, the Lennons were serious students of numerology. Rosen writes that once the Lennons were invited to a party that Greta Garbo and the Sheik of Saudi Arabia were scheduled to attend. "But Yoko said they couldn't go—it was out of the question. The numbers and the stars weren't right, particularly for her. It was going to be a traumatic February because of an eclipsed moon in her birth sign."

John seemed to have a natural affinity for understanding the significance of certain numbers, especially the number nine. Rosen lists many of those synchronicities.

- Both he and his second son Sean were born on October 9.

- Beatle song titles had the number nine in them, i.e. "One After 909" and "Revolution 9."

- The cover of John's Walls and Bridges album, which contains the song, "No. 9 Dream," is a drawing John did at age 11 which shows a soccer game with the number nine on one of the jerseys.

- Brian Epstein first saw the Beatles at The Cavern on November 9, 1961.

- John met Yoko on November 9.

- The Beatles' first recording contract was signed on May 9.

- John's mother Julia lived at 9 Newcastle Road.

Rosen writes that during John's years of seclusion, he studied Numerology with a passion. "It was just what he needed," Rosen says. "Numerology could quickly be applied to any situation to get a preliminary reading on the future . . . After learning about numerology, John and Yoko were unable to walk out of the house without finding mystical significance in every license plate, address, and street sign. They would not so much as dial a telephone number without first consulting their bible, *Cheiro's Book of Numbers*, which could have been subtitled *Numerology Made Easy*."

Yoko relied heavily on Charles Swan for psychic guidance. Rosen writes: "If Yoko was not at her desk when John woke up in the morning, he knew that she was downtown, in Soho, meeting with the O." Rosen says Swan earned every penny of his salary. "Yoko met with him or spoke to him seven days a week, for hours at a time, constantly calling him in the middle of the night. He did thousands of tarot readings.

Rosen says that Yoko was skilled at her own astrological and numerological calculations. "One of the reasons she and John chose to live at the Dakota was because the address—1 West 72nd Street, Apartment 72—had 'good numbers.'" The Lennons, Rosen writes:

> . . . didn't set foot outside the Dakota without first checking with the Oracle. Before they bought a house or an art object, O took a psychic reading. Did it give off evil vibrations? Was it a good investment? O acted as travel agent. He advised them where to go, the date of departure, the date of return. Was it safe to fly? Or was a voyage by sea a better idea? O told them whom to see and whom not to see; whom to do business with and whom not to do with business with; whom to hire and whom to fire. Sometimes they disagreed with him, but usually they followed his advice to the letter. If things didn't work out, Swan took the blame.

There was an end date to Swan's usefulness, according to Rosen. Speaking about John and Yoko's intent, Rosen says it wasn't to control the entire universe, but just see into the future on occasion to prepare themselves "for any nasty tricks the universe might hold in store. That's what the professional psychics were for. And they would remain on the payroll until John developed a consistently clear vision of the future, which Yoko believed was a strong possibility."

One of the most comforting aspects of past-life work for my clients has been the knowledge that they are not alone on this journey. They are part of a larger group of souls who've traveled together since creation. Our primary soul family is well aware of our short comings and desires, as they have been in the same lifetime with us over centuries, playing different roles and appearing in different genders. Your mother in this life could have been your husband in a previous life. Your wife could have been your brother.

When preparing for a particular incarnation, a lot of thought is given in our choice of parents. We take into consideration a number of factors, including the socio-economic conditions we will be born into. In making our selection of parents, we know ahead of time our race, creed and ethnicity. We pick parents who provide us with the environment we need to achieve our main objective, which is to resolve karmic issues we've brought in with us and most of all, to fulfill our soul's unique mission. Each parent is selected for the lessons they will provide that no other soul could do as well.

When I conduct a regression with the pre-life planning session, we spend time examining the role our parents play in helping us learn the lesson at hand—from abandonment to unconditional love and everything between. This includes any left-over issues from prior lifetimes we shared.

Once we decide on parents and have defined our soul's mission, other members of our soul family step up to announce whether they will come in with us, and if so, in what capacity and role. We choose each other often because of the love we shared in previous incarnations, but also because of the work we will do together. Because members of our soul family have an intimate knowledge of our soul's entire sojourn, they can zero in on whatever we need to learn. In that way, they can present challenges, or they can be supportive. You may wish that some of those souls never came into this life with you, but even those who create difficulties for you are doing so to help you in the long run. If you're working on the issue of abandonment, for instance, one or more of those souls may agree to come into your life with the sole purpose of abandoning you at some point in your life. In experiencing that lesson first hand, you will resolve the karma it created when it first occurred in a prior life and allow you to level the playing field so you don't have to deal with that ever again. It's often hard for us to see that what we perceive as a hurtful person in our lives, may actually be quite loving on a soul level. But no matter whether they come in as relatives, friends, teachers, neighbors, business associates or mentors, each has committed to playing a part in our soul's progress.

That is why when talking about a soul family, there are many, many souls interacting at various levels and at various points in time. They may be with you for your entire life, or they may come in and leave relatively quickly. The group can increase exponentially over time, but the core group remains small and intact from one life to the next.

While we are in the afterlife planning the next incarnation, we make covenants with those who will join us. The bond we share will draw us one to the other. Since there is nothing random in the universe, it is not surprising that the Beatles were drawn to each other and that everything fell into place to make their soul reunion happen. They shared a unique bond that transcended this earthly incarnation. I did not know it when I was in the midst of Beatlemania, but that realization became clearer and clearer as I began to understand how the universe operated.

Eric Meyers defines a soul group as "an assemblage of people drawn together to work through spiritual lessons. The Beatles had unresolved needs to perform and use artistry for broader cultural and spiritual reasons." Meyers says the group's core lesson "specifically involved the ongoing development of a spiritual message. In particular, the emphasis was on universal notions of love (in contrast to the initial demand for personality adoration and self-gain), spiritual awakening and a transpersonal perspective of reality. The developmental trajectory was to become writers

and messengers, serving as spiritual channels or conduits."
He later adds: "The songs developed into soundscapes,
while the lyrics grew to increasingly reflect spiritual ideas
and teachings. Also, there is the projection of the sacred
onto the group, and they have received their share of hero
worship and idealization."

While we are responsible for the design of an upcoming
life, and members of our soul family decide whether they
want to join us and what role they will subsequently play
in our attempt to achieve our soul's purpose, we can always
change our mind. Meyers acknowledges that the idea of
a destiny can be "a tricky concept for the personality to
grasp" and he factors in the role that astrology plays in that.

"Instead of predetermination another way to see destiny is the realization of soul intentions," he writes. " . . .
When John and Paul were first in the presence of each
other, the Moon was at the very same degree as they have
it in their relationship chart, a striking synchronicity. Addi-
tionally, the Moon was conjunct the Nodal Axis, which is
the signature of spiritual 'destiny.'"

The remembrance of a soul contract is often more on
a subconscious than a conscious level, although individuals
who revisit their pre-life planning session during a regression or meditation can clearly see their soul contract. This
is what happened to me and led me to write *Edgar Cayce
and the Unfulfilled Destiny of Thomas Jefferson Reborn*. It was
a book I reluctantly promised to write in my pre-life planning session. Once I incarnated and began remembering

my soul's mission in this life, there was a subliminal urge to get it down on paper and despite many obstacles I encountered along the way that would have given another soul pause to continue on that road, the urge I felt compelled me to keep at it for over eight years until it was finally published. In doing so, I fulfilled one of the clauses in my soul's contract.

There are hints that the same thing was in play for Paul. In looking at the astrology behind "Things We Said Today," Meyers says: "It's hypothesized the song revealed a soul contract, an agreement to remember a prior intention to reconnect during dreamtime."

George recognized the soul family connection between himself and the other three Beatles. According to Joshua Greene: "George saw his friendship with John, Paul, and Ringo as a continuation from past births. He quoted a lecture by Paramahansa Yogananda in which the kriya-yoga master described associations in this life as a carryover from previous lives."

The spiritual connection this contract set up continued long after their relationship soured. Referring to their strained relationship after John moved to New York, Rosen writes: "There appeared to be a psychic connection between John and Paul . . . every time McCartney was in town, John would hear Paul's music in his head."

George commented about the karmic connection between the Beatles. He understood there was a pattern in life and he believed everything was planned out in divine order. He extended that belief to include the path he was on with John, Paul and Ringo. Their interaction led to a reaction, so in essence, they were part of something everyone else was part of.

George would become, as Meyers states, "the spiritual conscience of the band, the most philosophical and thoughtful." For the rest of us, he would become the link between our old way of thinking to our more expansive thought system as he became, in Meyers' words, "a translator of spiritual principles into creative expression."

Paul also commented about the mystical way the four of them came together. Writing in *The Lyrics*, he says: ". . . I do often stop and wonder about the chances of the Beatles getting together . . . To this very day, it still is a complete mystery to me that it happened at all . . . All these small coincidences had to happen to make the Beatles happen, and it does feel like some kind of magic. It's one of the wonderful lessons about saying yes when life presents these opportunities to you. You never know where they could lead."

In John's 1980 *Playboy* interview, he drew on the Hindu concept of karma to express his thoughts about how personal relationships change over time. While he may have been thinking of a romantic relationship at the time, it could easily be applied to his relationship with the other Beatles:

> It's like what they say about karma. If you don't
> get it right in this lifetime, you have to come

back and go through it again. Well, those laws that are sort of cosmically talked about, accepted or not but talked about, apply down to the most minute detail of life, too. It's like 'Instant Karma,' which is my way of saying it, right? It's not just some big cosmic thing, although it's that as well, but it's also the same things, like your life here and your relationship with the person you want to live with and be with.

For George, it was a bit more complicated. Joshua Greene writes that since John, Paul, and Ringo had declined to join George on his spiritual journey, "the fabric that bound them as a team had come undone."

John understood that there was a reason certain souls were together. Certainly, he felt that way about Yoko. In his song, "Out The Blue," he describes her coming into his life: "I was born just to get to you." Yoko was certainly a part of the Beatles soul group, but she had a very specific role to play—one that did not earn her the love of Beatle fans.

Meyers comments about Yoko's energetic presence: "John brought Yoko into the sessions. It was tradition not to have wives or girlfriends in the studio, but John did not ask for permission. Geoff Emerick writes that he was "making it eminently clear that, like it or not, there was nothing they could do about it." From an energetic perspective, the addition of Yoko changes the dynamics. Though Yoko was never considered a member of the Beatles . . . Some argue that Yoko disrupted the group dynamic, contributing to the collapse. Certainly, the energetics with Yoko are different . . . There was resistance to accommodating her presence ... Feelings became activated and heated, perfect for potential catharsis. Yoko might have been the ideal catalyst for the necessary spiritual work."

Writing in *The Lyrics*, Paul acknowledges the role Yoko played. Talking about the period leading up to their breakup, he writes: "Yoko was literally in the middle of the recording session, and that was challenging. But it was also something we had to deal with. Unless there was a really serious problem—unless one of us said, 'I can't sing with her there'—we just had to let it be."

I could name many others who were members of the Beatles primary soul group, as it was a very large group indeed. Certainly John's mother Julia, and Paul's mother Mary, played a very big role in the trajectory of their sons' lives. Keeping in mind that John and Paul chose Julia and Mary as their mothers, it is not surprising that the early demise of both of their mothers created a series of circumstances which continued to influence their sons for many years. Paul was only fourteen when his mother died of cancer. He acknowledged the effect she had on his songwriting, acknowledging that she embodied the humanity that you might find in his songs.

The Maharishi Mahesh Yogi was another important member of the Beatles' soul group. Paul acknowledged that the Maharishi was the Beatles' spiritual advisor. No one can doubt the influence the Maharishi had on the group, especially where meditation and songwriting were concerned.

Looking at the Beatles, their relationships with each other, and the influence of their parents, siblings, wives, lovers, children, friends, mentors, business managers, etc., you can see each had a specific role to play in the scenario we called Beatlemania. Whether that role was the driving force behind the trajectory of their lives, or whether it played a minor role in impacting the path they chose, each in their own way did what they did as part of a greater plan—a plan we as fans became recipients of.

With all of this playing an essential role in the coming together and drifting apart of the Beatles, the singular underlying current impacting all four individually or as a group, is how all aspects of reincarnation revolve. Karma basically states that what you reap, so shall you sow. It's the universe's balancing act. You cannot be relieved of the consequences of your actions by merely going to confession. Somehow, someway, you answer for every thought, word and deed—whether from this life or a past life.

Each of the four Beatles were working on their own karmic debts. Many believe karma is always a bad thing, but it's not about good or bad. It's about cause and effect. Reap what you sow. Each of the Beatles brought in with them issues left unresolved from prior lives that they decided to work on in this life, and each of them brought in with them karmic attributes—things they mastered in prior lives. Karmic attributes are designed to aid a soul in resolving karmic issues brought in as unfinished business.

No one knows better than each of the Beatles what their karmic issues and attributes were all about. While there are individuals out there who claim to be readers or psychics who tell you about your past lives, my stance has always been that the best source of your past-life information is you. Every life you've ever lived can be replayed like a DVD. It's all stored in your soul. All you need to do is work with a reputable therapist to help you retrieve that information and focus on aspects of your soul's journey most in need of attention. I don't know if any of the Beatles ever sought out a past-life therapist and had a regression, so I don't know what their past-life issues were all about. But they left us with a lot of clues and several other authors have attempted to decipher what it was they may have been working on.

Meyers acknowledges that John and George were the Beatles most involved with spiritual exploration and that may have been because of actions taken in prior lifetimes. "Though becoming a 'mystic' is an ongoing and advanced process," Meyers writes of the two Beatles, "they brought a focus to the metaphysical and led the walking of this path. Their contributions were the most ethereal and pushed the envelope of experimentation, often with an exotic or cross-cultural orientation."

Meyers identifies John's main spiritual focus as the development of his leadership skills: "He had a karmic background of a visionary, a soul with big-picture perspectives and intuitive insight. He carried an unquenched desire to occupy visible positions to showcase his brilliance. He sought a career pushing innovative culture trends, wanting recognition for his talent . . . The spiritual work was to discover love within, a transformation into more joy and centeredness in the self."

Meyers referred to John's central soul intention as becoming a peace advocate: "specifically to use performance, arts and creativity to fulfill that aim. By so doing, he could finally 'win' his war and turn his karma inside-out."

Meyers writes that Paul's primary spiritual purpose is to "entertain the collective, in a very big way. He carries a pronounced need to be seen by the world, to become recognized and appreciated. He has the soul of a performer, and he has likely developed creative and artistic skill for many lifetimes." Meyers goes on to say that the central karmic issue in Paul's life "is the surrendering of his creative vision to handle necessary responsibilities. His ethic of responsibility (to the wishes of others, to help out financially) has undermined his ability to manifest his personal aims." Paul's spiritual lesson "is to become more healthily self-aligned, to rightfully develop leadership in realms of entertainment and smooth out his edge from karmic sacrifice." Despite his probable experience as a musician and entertainer in prior lifetimes, Meyers states that Paul was "unable to fully put it forth in the world, [consequently] in the present incarnation his innate musical talent developed easily, like tying his shoes."

Search no further than Ringo's name to get a hint about his purpose on earth. "He has a very deep and passionate need to perform and communicate through creative expression," Meyers writes. "It will be discussed as 'playful Ringo,' but this part of him hasn't always been able to shine. In fact, there is great angst, lots of intense and unsettled energy about sharing himself. The karmic lessons portray the reason for his frustrations. Ringo's central issue is loneliness. His chart speaks of isolation, the inability to connect with others and the resultant aggravation . . . Hanging in the balance of Ringo's spiritual lessons are substantial health issues, which contribute to the isolation and angst."

And then we come to George. According to Meyers, the central theme of George's chart is "bringing spirituality into public arenas through creative pursuits . . . The intention was to entertain, inspire, raise consciousness and deliver a message. The development of this promise hinged on his ability to resolve a complicated emotional pattern. George arrived into his life with an urgent need to make more loving contact with Spirit. He was clearing up the discord between dogmatic teachings and a much more compassionate and fluid experience of divinity. The karmic legacy of being hurt or disempowered by teachings has been taken personally, creating a component of fear in his psyche."

As I pointed out earlier in discussing members of one's soul family, George, like so many of us on our own spiritual journey, met individuals along the way who were instrumental in helping him pursue his path. Graeme Thomson credits Shankar as having introduced George to Tat Baba, Shankar's spiritual guru, "who explained the concept of karma, the cosmic law of action and reaction which posits that the soul is reborn again and again in different physical forms depending on its acts in a previous life."

Tillery quotes George from a conversation with Mukunda Goswami: "He (George) likened life to a piece of string with knots tied in it. The knots represent a person's karma from previous lives, and the object of a person's life is to untie the knots already there in order to be free. However, not being aware of that fact, people tend to create more knots while failing to untie the previous ones."[7]

George adds: "We have no one to blame but ourselves for the situation in which we now find ourselves, but on the other hand we can earn our way back to daylight in the future through positive actions now."

Tillery writes that: "It saddened Harrison that so few people grasped the truth he saw quite clearly—that we are here to burn out our past karma, to become aware of our divinity, to break free of eternal return."[8]

Karma was a topic George took seriously. Joshua Greene writes that George took to heart the advice he got from Prabhupada: "Your talent is not ordinary karma. It has a special purpose and Krishna will help you to fulfill it."

George recognized that everything that happened to the Beatles did so because of a confluence of karma. "We were made John, Paul, George and Ringo, because of what we did last time; it was all there for us, on a plate," he said. "We're reaping what we sowed in our last life, whatever it was. That's really all there is to it, Squire."

But George also knew he was working out his own karma. His wife Olivia acknowledges: "He had karma to work out, and he wasn't going to come back and be bad. He was going to be good and bad and loving and angry and everything all at once. You know, if someone said to you, 'Okay, you can go through your life and you can have everything in five lifetimes, or you can have a really intense one and have it in one, and then you can go and be liberated,' he would have said, 'Give me the one, I'm not coming back here.'"

Ever the teacher, in his book *I Me Mine*, George explained karma like this:

They say the thing about the chicken and the egg, and they don't know which comes first— and the seed growing into a tree, which produces seeds which grow into trees. This is Karma, the law of action-reaction— ('God is not mocked— for whatsoever a man soweth, that shall he also reap')—so every action has an equal and opposite reaction, which is like the chicken and the egg, each is a reaction to the other. And the only way you escape the chain of Karma, going round and round again, is if you get the seed and you roast it so it can't germinate (or fry the egg).

So, symbolically, the fire burns out the 'seed'. We have to first of all not create more Karma—that is, more actions and reactions—like throwing a pebble into a clear lake, the ripples keep on going. Every thought, word, action or deed that we have is like sending a ripple out across the Universe and it does eventually come back. Whatever you do, it comes right back on you.

The concept of self-responsibility was one that John echoed repeatedly. Churton writes:

"John Lennon was not a person who either welcomed or courted taking responsibility for other people's lives, quite understandably finding it sufficient a task in any given day to take responsibility for his own and close loved ones' existence and problems."

John seemed to have a keen understanding of karma. According to Churton, John believed "Anyone could be a Christ or a Hitler; they had to make a choice."

Tillery includes another quote from John on this topic: "Through engagement with the world you risked entanglement and defeat, and even if successful you achieved nothing that someone else couldn't achieve. The one thing you could do that absolutely no one else could do was to change yourself—to 'learn how to be you in time.'"[9]

It's interesting that often when I am asked to be a guest on a radio program, the host will play John's "Instant Karma" during the breaks. I'm actually honored, even though I know most hearing it don't know what it really means. Tillery speculates what that was: "The view that every person's actions have a ripple effect on the rest of humanity lies at the heart of his song 'Instant Karma (We all Shine On).' Tailoring the Hindu concept of karma to the here and now, he maintains that the cosmic laws of balance and consequences also apply in our current lives and relationships."[10]

David Bennahum, in his book, *In Their Own Words: the Beatles . . . after the Break-Up*, quotes an interview John gave just three days before his death, in which he went deeper into his thoughts about whether our actions are pre-ordained or if they are by our choice:

> Sometimes you wonder, I mean really wonder. I know we make our own reality and we always have a choice, but how much is pre-ordained? Is there always a fork in the road and are there two pre-ordained paths that are equally pre-ordained? There could be hundreds of paths where one could go this way or that way—there's a choice and it's very strange sometimes.

In that same interview, John went even further:

But for the few of us who did question what was going on . . . I have found out personally—not for the whole world! —that I am responsible for it, as well as them. I am part of them. There's no separation; we're all one, so in that respect, I look at it all and think, "Ah, well, I have to deal with me again in that way. What is real? What is the illusion I'm living or not living?" And I have to deal with it every day. The layers of the onion. But that is what it's all about.

John did not have to look any further than the evolution of the Beatles to know that everyone makes their own dreams come true. In his 1980 *Playboy* interview, John says:

> Produce your own dream . . . That's what the great masters and mistresses have been saying ever since time began. They can point the way, leave signposts and little instructions in various books that are now called holy and worshiped for the cover of the book and not what it says, but the instructions are all there for all to see, have always been and always will be . . . And people cannot provide it for you. I can't wake you up. *You* can wake you up. I can't cure you. *You* can cure you.

Gary Tillery writes:

> Lennon believed that humanity could reach a
> higher plane, that average men and women had
> it in their power to help reshape their culture in
> that direction if only they would recognize that
> capability. He devoted considerable effort to try-
> ing to make them aware of their power . . . As
> he suggested in 'All You Need Is Love,' Lennon
> believed that the key to achieving this state of
> affairs is self-transformation. The one thing each
> of us can do that absolutely no one else has the
> ability to do is change ourselves.[11]

So, what if we were to accept our karmic responsibility? Would the world be a different place? Tillery thinks so.
He raises the question:

> What if we accepted Lennon's assertions that nei-
> ther heaven, nor hell exist and that God is sim-
> ply the name for a naturally occurring force in
> the universe—a neutral powerhouse? Without
> the prospect of heaven or hell, we would have no
> expectation of reward or punishment after death.
> Would we suddenly descend to barbarism, rapine,
> and mayhem in the streets? Possibly. More likely
> we would simply focus better on our existence

here and now, being keenly aware of our transience and the wisdom of trying to live a full life.[12]

Over the years I have conducted many research projects into various aspects of past-life work, including life after death. I wanted to know what happens to us when we're in the afterlife between lives on Earth. What did we do there? How did our actions between lives set up the life we're leading now?

As I mentioned earlier, one of the common and consistent comments I've heard from clients over the years is their perception that someone or something, other than themselves, is responsible for what they are experiencing in this life. Yet self-responsibility is a theme in past-life work and one that George and John referred to throughout their later years.

Tillery writes: "Much of John Lennon's creative energy was expended on efforts to wake us up—to open our eyes to new possibilities and our own potential. Though he never characterized it as such himself, he was arguably calling for a new Enlightenment."[13]

In my opinion, one of the most hopeful lessons of reincarnation is that we have been all races, all genders, all nationalities, all religions, experiencing all socio-economic backgrounds, and living on every continent on the planet. If everyone truly believed that, it would be impossible to be judgmental about our fellow human beings because there, but for the Grace of God, go you.

John Lennon envisioned an ideal world in which, according to Tillery, "people would forgo violence and act out of sympathy and love. They would recognize that such traditional classifiers as religion, nationality, and skin color are meaningless from a cosmic perspective and that any other person should be treated simply as a fellow human being."[14]

Tillery goes on to say that: "While Lennon remained open minded about the possibility of life after death, he made his point of focus the here and now—how we can best use the quantum of time chance has allotted to us and what we can achieve as individuals and societies while we are still alive."[15]

And that's a good point, for every thought, word, and deed we have while we are alive is recorded in the Universe's super computer—the Akashic Record—and it is from there that our subsequent lifetimes are designed.

The idea of changing the world was not missed on George Harrison. Joshua Greene writes: "Prabhupada's first instruction to him at John Lennon's home had been that he could change the world by giving people knowledge about God, and for the past four years George had passionately followed that instruction, infusing his lyrics with descriptions of the soul, of an eternal universe beyond the covering of the material world, of a place the spirit can call home once escaping the cycle of reincarnation. The effort had not earned him much support from family or friends or from the press, and the shunning had led to sadness, the sadness to doubts."

Like most of us who specialize in one particular esoteric study, our interests are widespread and encompass many spiritual teachings. One of the things that surprised me when reading Eric Meyers' book, was when he relates what happened when the Beatles met Bob Dylan in a hotel room in New York. He called it, "a meeting of musical minds shaping Western culture." But it's what he says next that I had to read several times because it seemed so misplaced. Meyers says the conversation became philosophical at one point, "when Paul shared the insight that 'there are seven levels' to this existence, a notion John would make reference to in 'And Your Bird Can Sing' a couple years later." Where did *that* idea come from? Meyers says that while there's no agreement about there being seven levels, there is "almost universal consensus that there are various levels. Aside from physical, emotional and intellectual levels, most conceptualizations include a spiritual level (or levels). There are a multitude of definitions and perspectives on spirituality. The view here is non-denominational and universal—including the idea that the universe itself is alive, intelligent and in meaningful connection with everyone and everything. Imagine if it was possible to tap in to the spiritual dimension and understand the themes, issues and dynamics underlying the manifest world."

Kundalini energy was another area of spiritual interest, particularly for John. Kundalini is a form of divine energy, located at the base of the spine, which, when it rises and reaches the top of the head, the crown chakra, produces a spiritual awakening and a mystical experience that can be a profound transformation of consciousness. It can be achieved through meditation and yoga. Rosen writes that in John's "most optimistic, euphoric moods, he thought there was still a chance that the kundalini energy would shoot up his spine and that he'd levitate off the ground, at last becoming one with God."

John turned to yoga and meditation to achieve that level of consciousness. According to Rosen, the more John meditated, the more he began thinking about the path to enlightenment . . . once he merged with God, the wide range of psychic powers he'd develop would include not only clairvoyance, but also telepathy, the ability to fly through the air, and the ability to know of his past lives."

Well, I could have helped him with the latter!

Rosen believes that at one point, John considered his spiritual journey of more importance than the music business. "He needed to ascend to a higher spiritual plane," Rosen writes. "If he could develop his psychic powers, he'd be able to face life with newfound energies. It would be a true rebirth . . . Yoko assured John time and again that he could do anything he set his mind to, and that psychic powers were well within his reach. John agreed, aware that only prolonged meditation could arouse the 'kundalini' serpent energy at the base of his spine. The kundalini would then pass through his six centers of consciousness until it reached the seventh, located at the center of his brain. Only then would he be one with God. He'd know everything—past, present and future."

Rosen says John tapped the kundalini in flashes: "He could reach the fourth level of consciousness, located at the heart, almost at will. Then he could see the divine light, though he preferred to call it the Promised Land. He'd also been to the fifth level—location in the throat … Once he'd gone as high as the sixth level, located in his forehead."

Another study that falls into this category is astrology. While I know very little about it, there is no doubt in my mind that it works hand-in-hand with other metaphysical laws. Meyers said that in the sixties, "the astrological weather emphasized the process of spiritual awakening" and that "The Beatles served as musical conduits who expressed the energetic themes of their day."

Meyers also states that the "Beatles became open to and interested in astrology, reportedly having an inhouse astrologer at their Apple location. Yoko Ono has been an astrology enthusiast for years and it was a part of her relationship with John. "John had a pileup of planets in his astrological area of mysticism, consciousness and transcendence," Meyers writes. "The inspirational and metaphysical dimensions were abundant, but there were also psychological facets as well."

Rosen writes that "the Lennons ran their lives by the zodiac and Mercury Retrograde charts." John followed British astrologer Patric Walker's horoscopes in *Town &*

Country magazine. "Every month he clipped Libra for himself and Aquarius for Yoko," Rosen writes. "Underlining significant passages, he correlated them with upcoming events, scribbling notes of warning or things to look forward to. At the end of the month, he reviewed his findings. Never did he declare the horoscope itself inaccurate. The only inaccuracies were in his interpretations."

According to Rosen, Yoko taught John everything he needed to know about Mercury Retrograde. This is the time of year when the planet Mercury appears to move backwards in the sky and for three weeks, everything that can go wrong, will go wrong. "John hated and feared these tri-annual episodes as much as Yoko did, or at least he pretended to," Rosen wrote. "As Mercury Retrograde neared, he'd count down the days, then try to deal with it as best he could according to Mother's (Yoko's) rules of astrology, tarot and numerology. As far as Yoko was concerned, when Mercury kicked in, the only thing to do was nothing, preferably in a house that faced the right direction. You can't fight Mercury Retrograde. Nothing will be accomplished."

George was also immersed in the subject matter. On his posthumous album *Brainwashed,* he sang of being a "Pisces Fish." On George's visit to India to study sitar with Ravi Shankar, Meyers writes: "The astrology between the men illustrates a mentor/apprentice dynamic in spiritual pursuits. Ravi played an important role in George's philosophical development, the healing of his prior wounding with dogma. He challenged George to live authentically and forge new directions. It's astounding that the lead guitarist of the world's most successful rock band would devote himself to an obscure Indian instrument at the band's peak."

Paul mentions astrology in relation to his song, "Hello Goodbye," which plays on the theme of duality—relating it to his Sun sign Gemini. Paul talks about his Sun sign in his book, *The Lyrics*. "With Gemini you're born in the middle of the year, so there's all that bit of the year gone and there's all this bit of the year to come and you are born slap bang in the middle," he writes. "I definitely have this yin-yang thing . . . ebony and ivory; hello and goodbye; you say yes, I say no. Often I'm playing with that sense of dichotomy."

In discussing "Eleanor Rigby," Meyers said that many years after he wrote that song, Paul was informed that the real Eleanor Rigby was buried in a cemetery near where he met John at the garden fete in Liverpool. "Paul attributes the "coincidence" to his subconscious," Meyers writes. "Exactly! Paul has an uncanny ability to intuit from other dimensions . . . Coincidences are better understood as synchronicities, how the psyche is meaningfully connected to a vast matrix of consciousness—the very same intelligent organizational matrix of astrology. And it is through astrology we see the deeper meaning of the actual Eleanor Rigby."

Meyers has a section in his book in which he discusses the origin of the name, The Beatles, and how the group originally was called "The Beetles," and "The Silver Beetles." He shared the importance of beetles to the ancient Egyptian culture, a culture that lay the groundwork for much of our modern metaphysical philosophies.

"For the Egyptians, beetles were thought to use the lofty position to fly into the celestial planes and bring back messages," Meyers writes, adding that this was "a theme with these musicians." He goes on to write: "The scarab beetle was famously part of Carl Jung's fascination with synchronicity—the insect appearing on his office window when a client was mentioning its appearance in a dream. Like the Egyptians, he discussed the scarab in his Red Book as the "classical rebirth symbol," linking the insect with eternality and transformation."

And certainly, when stepping back and looking at the Beatle years in their entirety, we can see the tremendous transformational opportunities the group provided for the world. Eric Meyers captures that sentiment when he writes: "It turns out that the Beatles example has relevance to us all—a remarkable coming of age story depicting universal themes of spiritual development, even including important teachings. Whether they were conscious of it or not, their story and music incredibly portray stages of growth, paralleling the astrology of their time. They exemplified spiritual discovery, while making a terrific soundtrack about it too!"

Eric Meyers writes: "Spiritual awakening has been compared to a seed that blossoms into a flower. The point is not to leave the personality (seed), but to have it mature and radiate the soulful beauty (flowering) which envelops and sustains us."

Murray Silver, author of *Great Balls of Fire*, who had also been a photographer for the Dark Horse tour in 1974 and had spent days asking George about his spiritual interests, echoes the same idea. Joshua Greene reports that Silver was asked if he thought George had been trying too hard to get a message through. "Maybe at first," he said, "but from what I saw of him, he was just trying to put information out there and hoping it would take root. He was planting seeds. That's all the man was doing. Planting seeds. He was hoping that one day the clues would blossom into something."

Something, indeed!

Afterword

As with any deep dive into one's past, the research I conducted for this book was cathartic in more ways than one. It chronicled my evolution as I struggled with my identity in a world shaped by the events of the sixties, the socioeconomic environment I was raised in, and the coming of age with a band whose influence would determine the trajectory of my soul's path. I once again came face-to-face with the people, places and things that shaped who I am today. In the end, did it answer that burning question I raised at the beginning of the book? How did a young girl from an Italian-American Catholic family growing up in the sixties on Chicago's southside become so immersed in the world of esoteric philosophies? Did my teenage obsession with the Beatles have anything to do with it? I can answer that question now with a resounding YES!

I looked over the last sixty years from several perspectives. The first was as a young teenage girl dealing with loss, yearning to belong to a family of like-minded souls, navigating the spiritual challenges brought on by twelve years of Catholic schooling and the social challenges of living in the turbulent sixties. It is very much a coming-of-age story. Then there's the viewpoint of a Beatles fan turned Beatles fan club president who became entangled in the David and Goliath-size battle over the autonomy of the fan clubs. And finally, it's the story of a young woman who emerged from those years, scared with a few wounds, but armed with the very talents, skills and abilities that would eventually lead her to a career as a reincarnation specialist, author, and speaker.

If I knew then what I know now, I would have looked upon those years from a totally different perspective—more as a training ground than a battle field. I would have paid greater attention to the message George was trying to convey instead of being so judgmental about the culture he embraced that was so foreign to me. I would have taken my studies more seriously and perhaps launched my career much sooner than it actually materialized. That being said, however, I know that it is only when the student is ready that the teacher appears. Lessons needed to be learned. Everything had to play itself out in its own time.

From a reincarnation standpoint, it all makes sense. Everything that I experienced was a stepping stone to what was next. Reliving some of those cringe-worthy experiences was painful, but I learned to forgive myself. After all, I was just a kid and learning on the job what it meant to be diplomatic and resourceful, while taking a stab at implementing conflict resolution. The questioning of my religious upbringing led me to explore other spiritual beliefs and stumble upon the esoteric philosophies that would later define my life. So many factors were at play, but in the midst of it all, there were the Beatles. From the moment they entered my life in February 1964, they opened the floodgates for me emotionally, mentally, and most importantly, spiritually. Their music tore down the wall of negative self-talk that surrounded me and made me believe in myself. They gave me the courage to explore philosophical theories far outside my comfort zone. They instilled in me a passionate belief in something that most in my circle considered to be outside the box, and yet once embraced, I never wavered.

I am eternally grateful to John, Paul, Ringo, and especially to George, for illuminating the path that has led me to a career that continues to excite and inspire me. I am humbled by the role I have in providing a service to those who find their way to me, yearning to understand why they are here and what special purpose their soul has in this school we call Mother Earth. Whether it is through a past-life regression to learn how the past is impacting the present, or exploring how Soul Writing can be used to provide answers to life's most profound questions, I am privileged to be a conduit that empowers and inspires each soul I meet.

Yes, the Beatles truly sparked that "Inner Light" within me and thousands of others "across the universe." I hope in reading this book, it did the same for you.

—*Joanne DiMaggio*
November 2023

Addendum

How To Do Soul Writing™

Soul Writing™ is a written form of meditation. It is you going into a meditative state through deep breathing and total relaxation, putting the pen to paper, and having a conversation with God, your Higher Self (Soul), Angels, Ascended Masters, Muse, or other divine emissaries. It is a 24-7 hotline, providing loving guidance on any issues facing you. It answers the "why" questions we all ask in a time of spiritual or physical crisis. Soul Writing is something anyone can do—most get something on the first try. This form of meditative writing provides you with a profound connection to the Divine within, to the core of your being, and enables you to tap into the collective consciousness where answers to all of life's—and death's—questions can be found.

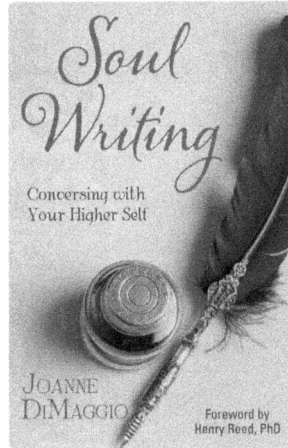

Here are a few steps to get your started:

- **Find a sacred place.** Walk through your home and find your own sacred writing space with the aesthetic qualities most conducive to your connection to Spirit.

- **Set the stage.** Surround yourself with items that remind you of your spiritual journey, such as music, artwork, crystals, candles, incense, etc.

- **Same time. Same place.** Humans are creatures of habit. If you consistently write at the same time and in the same place, you condition yourself to connect that much quicker.

- **Pen versus the keyboard.** It's a matter of preference. Experiment with both. However, keep in mind that since you close your eyes halfway when doing this writing, if you are on a keyboard and are one key off, you may not be able to read the message afterwards.

- **Meditation is Key.** A silent entering into a peaceful state is essential.

- **Say a Prayer of Protection.** Picture yourself surrounded by a bubble of bright, white light. Say a prayer of protection, asking that you be kept safe from all things seen and unseen that is not for your highest and best. Do not skip this step. *"Mother. Father. God. I ask that the divine* *light that emanates from the essence of your being descend upon me, surrounding me with an iridescent aura, protecting me from all things seen and unseen that are opposition to my greater good. I ask it and so it is."*

- **Focus on a question.** Think about whatever is troubling you and form a precise question about it. The more profound the question—the more profound the answer—so give this some thought. If you do not have a specific question, ask for a message for your highest and best.

- **Get Ready to Write!** Allow the pen to be poised over the paper and rest loosely in your hand. Start with ovals and loops to get the ink flowing until words, phrases and sentences form. If you get nothing on paper, but hear something in your head, write that down and go back to ovals.

- **Allow the Message to Proceed.** Do not edit for punctuation, grammar or spelling. This is stream of consciousness writing. You can 'fix it' later.

- **Wait Before you Read.** Writing is like a fine wine. It improves with age and takes on a completely different meaning in the weeks, months and years ahead.

- **Keep Your Writing Safe!** Soul Writing is a sacred contract between you and the Divine. Share what you feel is generic, but keep personal information to yourself.

Bibliography

Atwater, P.M.H., L.H.D. *Coming Back to Life: Examining the After-Effects of the Near-Death Experience.* Kill Devil Hills, NC. Transpersonal Publishing. 2008.

Bennahum, David. *In Their Own Words. The Beatles . . . After the Break-Up.* London. Omnibus Press. 1991.

Berman, Garry. *"We're Going to See the Beatles!" An Oral History of Beatlemania as Told by the Fans Who Were There.* Santa Monica, CA. Santa Monica Press. 2008.

Bernstein, Morey. *The Search for Bridey Murphy.* New York, NY. Doubleday. 1956.

Blake, John. *All You Needed Was Love: The Beatles After the Beatles.* New York, NY. Perigee Books. 1981.

Brown, Peter and Gaines, Steven. *The Love You Make: An Insider's Story of The Beatles.* New York, NY. New American Library. 2002.

Chiu, David. *The Beatles in India: 16 Things You Didn't Know.* Rolling Stone. February 2021.

Churton, Tobias. *The Spiritual Meaning of the Sixties. The Magic, Myth & Music of the Decade That Changed the World.* Rochester, VT. Inner Traditions. 2018.

Comfort, Ray. *The Beatles, God & The Bible.* Washington, DC. WND Books. 2012.

DiMaggio, Joanne, MA, Cht. *Edgar Cayce and the Unfulfilled Destiny of Thomas Jefferson Reborn.* Huntsville, AR. Ozark Mountain Publishing. 2020.

DiMaggio, Joanne, MA, Cht. *Soul Writing: Conversing with Your Higher Self.* Charlottesville, VA. Olde Souls Press. 2011.

Feldman-Barrett, Christine. *A Women's History of the Beatles.* New York, NY. Bloomsbury Publishing, Inc. 2021.

Giuliano, Geoffrey. *Blackbird: The Life and Times of Paul McCartney.* New York, NY. Penguin Books. 1991.

Giuliano, Geoffrey. *Dark Horse. The Private Life of George Harrison.* New York, NY. Penguin Books. 1989.

Greene, Joshua M. *Here Comes The Sun: The Spiritual and Musical Journey of George Harrison.* Hoboken, NJ. John Wiley & Sons, Inc. 2006.

Harrison, George. *I Me Mine.* Guildford, England. Genesis Publications Ltd. 1980.

Harrison, Olivia. *George Harrison: Living in the Material World.* Abrams, NY. Harry N. Abrams. 2011.

Hill, Christopher. *Into the Mystic: The Visionary and Ecstatic Roots of 1960s Rock and Roll.* Rochester, VT. Park Street Press. 2017.

Kahn, Ashley. *George Harrison on George Harrison: Interviews and Encounters.* Chicago, IL. Chicago Review Press. 2020.

Leonard, Candy. *Beatleness How the Beatles and Their Fans Remade the World*. New York, NY. Arcade Publishing. 2014.

Lewisohn, Mark. *Tune In. The Beatles: All These Years. Vol. 1*. New York, NY. Crown Publishing. 2013.

MacDonald, Ian. *Revolution in the Head: The Beatles' Record and the Sixties*. Chicago, IL. Chicago Review Press. 2007.

Mancuso, Pat Kinzer. *Do You Promise Not To Tell? The Final Story of the Official George Harrison Fan Club*. Hamburg, Germany. Tredition. 2021.

Martin, George, with Jeremy Hornsby. *All You Need is Ears: The Inside Personal Story of the Genius Who Created The Beatles*. New York, NY. St. Martin's Griffin. 1979.

McCartney, Paul. *Paul McCartney: The Lyrics. 1956 to Present*. New York, NY. Liverlight Publishing Corporation. 2021.

Miles, Barry. *Beatles In Their Own Words*. London. Omnibus Press. 1978.

Meyers, Eric, M.A. *The Spiritual Dimension of the Beatles*. Camas, WA. Astrology Site Publishing. 2021.

Rosen, Robert. *Nowhere Man. The Final Days of John Lennon*. Oakland, CA. Quick American Archives. 2002.

Saltzman, Paul. *The Beatles in India*. San Rafael, CA. Insight Editions. 2018.

Schaffner, Nicholas. *The Beatles Forever*. New York, NY. McGraw-Hill. 1977.

Schmidt, Sara. *Dear Beatle People: The Story of the Beatles North American Fan Club.* Houston, TX. Texas Book Publishers Association. 2023.

Snow, Mat. *The Beatles Solo: George Harrison. The Illustrated Chronicles of John, Paul, George, and Ringo After the Beatles.* New York, NY. Race Point Publishing. 2013.

Thomson, Graeme. *George Harrison Behind the Locked Door.* New York. NY. Omnibus Press. 2015.

Tillery, Gary. *The Cynical Idealist. A Spiritual Biography of John Lennon.* Wheaton, IL. Theosophical Publishing House. 2009.

Tillery, Gary. *Working Class Mystic: A Spiritual Biography of George Harrison.* Wheaton, IL. Theosophical Publishing House. 2011.

Turner, Steve. *A Hard Day's Write. The Stories Behind Every Beatles Song.* New York, NY. Harper Collins Publishers, Inc. 1994.

Endnotes

Introduction

[1] *Working Class Mystic: A Spiritual Biography of George Harrison*, Gary Tillery, ©2011, p. 151. *This material was reproduced by permission of Quest Books, the imprint of The Theosophical Publishing House (www.questbooks.net).*

[2] *Working Class Mystic: A Spiritual Biography of George Harrison*, Gary Tillery, ©2011, pp. 113-114. *This material was reproduced by permission of Quest Books, the imprint of The Theosophical Publishing House (www.questbooks.net).*

Chapter One

[1] *The Cynical Idealist: A Spiritual Biography of John Lennon*, Gary Tillery, ©2009, pp. 53-54. *This material was reproduced by permission of Quest Books, the imprint of The Theosophical Publishing House (www.questbooks.net).*

[2] *Working Class Mystic: A Spiritual Biography of George Harrison*, Gary Tillery, ©2011, p. 154. *This material was reproduced by permission of Quest Books, the imprint of The Theosophical Publishing House (www.questbooks.net).*

[3] *Working Class Mystic: A Spiritual Biography of George Harrison*, Gary Tillery, ©2011, p. 37. *This material was reproduced by permission of Quest Books, the imprint of The Theosophical Publishing House (www.questbooks.net).*

[4] *The Cynical Idealist: A Spiritual Biography of John Lennon*, Gary Tillery, ©2009, pp. 46. This material was reproduced by permission of Quest Books, the imprint of The Theosophical Publishing House (www.questbooks.net).

[5] *The Cynical Idealist: A Spiritual Biography of John Lennon*, Gary Tillery, ©2009, p. 4. This material was reproduced by permission of Quest Books, the imprint of The Theosophical Publishing House (www.questbooks.net).

Chapter Four

[1] *Working Class Mystic: A Spiritual Biography of George Harrison*, Gary Tillery, ©2011, p. 35. This material was reproduced by permission of Quest Books, the imprint of The Theosophical Publishing House (www.questbooks.net).

[2] *Working Class Mystic: A Spiritual Biography of George Harrison*, Gary Tillery, ©2011, p. 58. This material was reproduced by permission of Quest Books, the imprint of The Theosophical Publishing House (www.questbooks.net).

Chapter Nine

[1] *Working Class Mystic: A Spiritual Biography of George Harrison*, Gary Tillery, ©2011, p. 46. This material was reproduced by permission of Quest Books, the imprint of The Theosophical Publishing House (www.questbooks.net).

[2] *Working Class Mystic: A Spiritual Biography of George Harrison*, Gary Tillery, ©2011, pp. 128-129. This material was reproduced by permission of Quest Books, the imprint of The Theosophical Publishing House (www.questbooks.net).

[3] *The Cynical Idealist: A Spiritual Biography of John Lennon*, Gary Tillery, ©2009, pp. 46-47. This material was reproduced by

permission of Quest Books, the imprint of The Theosophical Publishing House (www.questbooks.net).

[4] *The Cynical Idealist: A Spiritual Biography of John Lennon, Gary Tillery,* ©*2009, p. 69. This material was reproduced by permission of Quest Books, the imprint of The Theosophical Publishing House (www.questbooks.net).*

[5] *The Cynical Idealist: A Spiritual Biography of John Lennon, Gary Tillery,* ©*2009, p. 137. This material was reproduced by permission of Quest Books, the imprint of The Theosophical Publishing House (www.questbooks.net).*

[6] *The Cynical Idealist: A Spiritual Biography of John Lennon, Gary Tillery,* ©*2009, pp. 147-148. This material was reproduced by permission of Quest Books, the imprint of The Theosophical Publishing House (www.questbooks.net).*

[7] *Working Class Mystic: A Spiritual Biography of George Harrison, Gary Tillery,* ©*2011, p. 110. This material was reproduced by permission of Quest Books, the imprint of The Theosophical Publishing House (www.questbooks.net).*

[8] *Working Class Mystic: A Spiritual Biography of George Harrison, Gary Tillery,* ©*2011, p. 150. This material was reproduced by permission of Quest Books, the imprint of The Theosophical Publishing House (www.questbooks.net).*

[9] *The Cynical Idealist: A Spiritual Biography of John Lennon, Gary Tillery,* ©*2009, p. 57. This material was reproduced by permission of Quest Books, the imprint of The Theosophical Publishing House (www.questbooks.net).*

[10] *The Cynical Idealist: A Spiritual Biography of John Lennon*, Gary Tillery, ©2009, p.140. This material was reproduced by permission of Quest Books, the imprint of The Theosophical Publishing House (www.questbooks.net).

[11] *The Cynical Idealist: A Spiritual Biography of John Lennon*, Gary Tillery, ©2009, p. 136. This material was reproduced by permission of Quest Books, the imprint of The Theosophical Publishing House (www.questbooks.net).

[12] *The Cynical Idealist: A Spiritual Biography of John Lennon*, Gary Tillery, ©2009, p. 152. This material was reproduced by permission of Quest Books, the imprint of The Theosophical Publishing House (www.questbooks.net).

[13] *The Cynical Idealist: A Spiritual Biography of John Lennon*, Gary Tillery, ©2009, p. 8. This material was reproduced by permission of Quest Books, the imprint of The Theosophical Publishing House (www.questbooks.net).

[14] *The Cynical Idealist: A Spiritual Biography of John Lennon*, Gary Tillery, ©2009, p. 138. This material was reproduced by permission of Quest Books, the imprint of The Theosophical Publishing House (www.questbooks.net).

[15] *The Cynical Idealist: A Spiritual Biography of John Lennon*, Gary Tillery, ©2009, p. 138. This material was reproduced by permission of Quest Books, the imprint of The Theosophical Publishing House (www.questbooks.net).

About the Author

Joanne DiMaggio, MA, CHt, has been professionally pursuing past-life research, therapy, and Soul Writing™for 35 years. She has been actively involved with Edgar Cayce's Association for Research and Enlightenment (A.R.E.). since 1987, and she earned her Masters in Transpersonal Studies and her Spiritual Mentor certification through Atlantic University. Joanne has written numerous articles, spoken at many conferences, and has been a guest on over 100 radio programs and podcasts. She is the author of *Soul Writing, Your Soul Remembers, Karma Can Be a Real Pain, I Did It To Myself . . . Again!,* and *Edgar Cayce and the Unfulfilled Destiny of Thomas Jefferson Reborn.* Find out more at www.joannedimaggio.com.

Rainbow Ridge Books publishes spiritual, metaphysical, and self-help titles. To contact authors and editors, peruse our titles, and see submission guidelines, please visit our website at www.rainbowridgebooks.com.